Echoes of the Union

The FSU Tragedy and Its Aftermath

Table of Content

Introduction 1

    Overview of the Incident 1

    Contextualizing the Tragedy 1

    Purpose of the Book 2

    Structure of the Book 2

Part I 4

Chapter 1 Life at the Student Union 5

    Daily Routines, Student Life, and the Role of the Union at FSU .6

    The Social and Cultural Hub of Campus Life 7

    How the Union Shapes FSU's Identity 9

Chapter 2 Who Was Phoenix Ikner? 12

    Background, Upbringing, and Family Dynamics 13

    Phoenix's Early Life and Education 15

    Psychological Profile and Early Warning Signs 17

Chapter 3 Warning Signs and Missed Moments 19

    Behavioral Red Flags Leading Up to the Incident 20

    Social Media Posts and Their Ignored Significance ... 22

    How Friends, Family, and Staff Failed to Act 23

Chapter 4 Access and Accountability 26

How the Shooter Obtained the Weapon 27

Legal and Institutional Gaps in Firearm Access 29

The Role of Gun Laws and Their Impact on Campus Safety 32

Part II 35

Chapter 5 Warning Signs and Missed Moments 36

Detailed Breakdown of the Shooting Event 37

Key Moments and Decisions Leading to the Tragedy 39

The Impact of the Shooter's Actions on the Campus Community
.... 41

Chapter 6 Voices in Chaos: Eyewitness Accounts 43

Testimonies from Students, Faculty, and First Responders 44

The Role of Bystanders and Their Impact on the Situation 46

Coping Mechanisms and Emotional Responses During the Crisis
.... 48

Chapter 7 Campus Security and Law Enforcement 52

Reactions from Authorities During the Incident 53

How Law Enforcement Prevented Further Losses 55

Evaluating the Effectiveness of Campus Security Protocols 58

Part III 61

Chapter 8 Lives Lost and Lives Changed 62

A Tribute to Victims and Their Stories 63

Survivors' Accounts and the Road to Recovery 65

The Lasting Impact on Families and Friends of the Victims 67

Chapter 9 The Mourning Campus: Vigils and Solidarity .. 70

Community Responses, Memorials, and National Support 71

Healing through Collective Grief and Remembrance 73

The Role of Social Media in Organizing Memorial Events 75

Chapter 10 Law Enforcement Under Scrutiny 78

Personal and Professional Responsibilities in the Aftermath 79

Investigations into Law Enforcement's Handling of the Crisis .. 82

Reforms and Training After the Tragedy 84

Chapter 11 Mental Health and Responsibility 88

The Role of Mental Health in Prevention and Accountability ... 89

The Importance of Early Intervention and Support Systems 92

Addressing Stigma and Promoting Mental Health Awareness on Campus 94

Part IV 97

Chapter 12 Guns and Campuses: A National Debate Rekindled 98

Renewed Discussions on Gun Laws Post-Tragedy 99

Debates on Campus Safety and Legal Responsibility 102

The Role of Political Advocacy Groups in Shaping Policy..... 104

Chapter 13 Rebuilding Trust and Security at FSU 107

Institutional Changes and Student Safety Reforms 108

The Role of Counseling and Support Services in Campus Recovery 111

Revisiting FSU's Emergency Response Protocols................... 113

Chapter 14 Resilience in Red and Gold.............................. 117

Inspirational Stories of Unity and Activism 118

The Strength of FSU's Student Body and Faculty in Overcoming Tragedy 120

How FSU Students Are Leading Efforts for Change 123

Chapter 15 From Tragedy to Advocacy................................. 126

How Survivors and Families Are Using Their Voices to Drive Change.. 127

Legislative Efforts to Prevent Future Tragedies 128

The Role of Advocacy Groups in Fostering Public Awareness 131

Part V 135

Chapter 16 Echoes Across America... 136

The National Impact and Parallels with Other School Shootings 137

The Growing Movement for Gun Control and School Safety Reform 139

How Other Universities Are Responding to Similar Tragedies 142

Epilogue The Union Remains 145

Final Reflections on Grief, Resilience, and Creating Safer Campuses 146

The Legacy of FSU's Resilience and the Continuing Efforts for Change 148

Looking Toward a Future of Healing and Protection 149

Introduction

Overview of the Incident

On April 17, 2025, Florida State University (FSU) was forever changed by a tragic event that shocked the campus and the world. A mass shooting occurred at the university's Student Union, a vibrant hub of student life, claiming the lives of multiple victims and leaving many others injured. The shooter, Phoenix Ikner, a former student, unleashed violence in an area typically associated with safety and connection. The tragedy set off an immediate response from law enforcement, first responders, and the FSU community, as the violence reverberated through the hearts of students, faculty, and families alike. This book explores the events surrounding the shooting, the aftermath, and the larger societal issues that were brought into sharp focus.

Contextualizing the Tragedy

This tragedy is not an isolated event. The shooting at FSU is part of a troubling trend of school shootings that have been occurring across the United States. It brings attention to the ongoing debates about gun laws, mental health, campus security, and how society addresses the underlying causes of such violence. In a world where mass shootings seem to be an increasingly common tragedy, the FSU shooting serves as a reminder that no campus, no community, is immune. The book contextualizes this tragedy within broader discussions about the safety of students, the accessibility of firearms, and the mental health support systems in place (or lack thereof) within educational institutions. It also reflects on the devastating emotional toll such events have on the families of the victims, the survivors, and the larger community.

Purpose of the Book

The purpose of this book is to delve deeply into the FSU tragedy, examining the incident from multiple angles. It is not merely an account of what happened, but a comprehensive exploration of how such events occur and the long-lasting effects they have. Through this book, we aim to shed light on the experiences of those directly involved—the victims, survivors, and the university community—as well as the responses from law enforcement and the public. We also explore the importance of healing and reform, asking critical questions about the role of mental health, gun control, and campus safety in preventing future tragedies. This book ultimately seeks to honor the memory of the victims while advocating for meaningful change in how we approach issues of violence, safety, and security on campuses across the nation.

Structure of the Book

This book is divided into five parts, each focusing on different aspects of the FSU tragedy and its aftermath:

Part I Before the Echo: This section examines life at FSU before the tragedy struck, providing insights into the student union's role in campus life, the background of the shooter, and the missed signs leading up to the incident.

Part II The Day Everything Changed: In this section, we chronicle the events of April 17, 2025, offering a detailed timeline of the shooting and the chaos that ensued. We also share the perspectives of those who witnessed the horror firsthand.

Part III Aftermath and Reckoning: Following the shooting, this section addresses the immediate responses, both from law enforcement and the FSU community, and the ongoing debates about accountability and the lessons learned.

Part IV Toward Healing and Change: This section focuses on the efforts to rebuild trust, promote healing, and enact policy reforms at FSU and beyond. It also highlights the resilience of the survivors and the advocacy for stronger campus security and mental health resources.

Part V The National Impact: The final section examines how the FSU tragedy sparked national conversations about gun control, campus safety, and the need for policy reforms at universities across the country.

Part I

Before the Echo

Chapter 1
Life at the Student Union

The Student Union at Florida State University (FSU) serves as the heart of campus life, playing a pivotal role in shaping the daily experiences of students. This vibrant hub is where students gather to study, socialize, engage in extracurricular activities, and connect with the university's diverse community. It is more than just a physical space; it is the nucleus of student life, providing a sense of belonging and purpose. Through its various facilities, services, and events, the Union supports the academic, social, and emotional needs of the students. From hosting club meetings to providing resources for student organizations, the Union acts as a catalyst for student engagement, fostering leadership and collaboration.

The Union is also a place where the university's social and cultural diversity comes to life. Students from various backgrounds come together to exchange ideas, celebrate their traditions, and create new shared experiences. The Union hosts events that represent the rich tapestry of FSU's community, including cultural performances, guest lectures, and social events that bring people together. It serves as a bridge for students to connect with each other and with the broader university community, enhancing the campus experience for all.

Beyond just a social and cultural space, the Union plays a significant role in shaping FSU's identity. It represents the values and mission of the university, emphasizing inclusivity, diversity, and student empowerment. As a landmark institution on campus, the Union embodies the spirit of FSU, reflecting its commitment to providing a supportive and dynamic environment where students can thrive academically, socially, and personally. In many ways, the Student Union is not just a building, but a living, breathing reflection of what it means to be a part of the FSU community.

Daily Routines, Student Life, and the Role of the Union at FSU

The Student Union at Florida State University (FSU) plays an integral role in the daily routines and overall student life, making it one of the most central and important locations on campus. For many students, the Union serves as a daily destination—whether for grabbing a quick bite to eat, attending a club meeting, or simply finding a quiet space to study. The building is a key part of the rhythm of student life, providing both a functional and social environment where students can balance their academic responsibilities with the need for personal connection and relaxation.

Each day at FSU begins with students heading to the Union for their morning routines. Whether it's picking up coffee from one of the Union's cafés or meeting up with friends before class, the space is alive with activity. For students who live off-campus, the Union serves as a convenient and central location for accessing essential services, including financial aid, student government offices, and the career center. The Union's central location makes it a perfect meeting point for students, professors, and staff alike, contributing to the university's sense of community. In the mornings, you'll find students grabbing breakfast, studying in the quiet areas, or preparing for the day's events. The Union's role in the daily routines of students is essential to the flow of campus life, ensuring that students have a hub to connect with each other and with resources that aid their academic success.

Throughout the day, the Union comes alive with diverse student activities. The building is home to a wide range of student organizations, events, and programming that enhance the college experience. Whether it's a meeting for one of FSU's many student clubs, a cultural event, or an educational lecture, the Union's rooms and event spaces are constantly in use. This contributes to a rich and varied student life, where students are encouraged to engage in extracurricular activities and pursue their interests outside of the classroom. From leadership programs to advocacy groups, the Union facilitates opportunities for students to get involved in the greater FSU community.

The Social and Cultural Hub of Campus Life

The Union is more than just a place to eat, meet, or study. It is a cornerstone of student life, offering students the opportunity to become engaged members of their university community. Through its variety of services, resources, and programs, the Union supports FSU's mission to foster student success, involvement, and well-being. It embodies the spirit of student life at FSU, playing a vital role in creating a dynamic and supportive environment where students can thrive academically, socially, and personally.

The Student Union at Florida State University (FSU) is more than just a place for students to gather between classes; it is a vibrant social and cultural hub that plays a critical role in shaping the campus community. At its core, the Union is a space where the diverse student body comes together, fostering a sense of inclusion, belonging, and connection among students from all backgrounds. It is the epicenter of student life, where academic, social, and cultural experiences converge, and where students find opportunities to engage with each other and the broader world.

FSU's Student Union provides a space for students to celebrate their cultural identities, share their traditions, and learn from one another. With a variety of student organizations, cultural events, and performances held regularly, the Union is constantly buzzing with activity that showcases the rich diversity of FSU's student body. Events like international cultural nights, heritage month celebrations, and art exhibitions create an environment where students are encouraged to explore and embrace the cultural backgrounds of their peers. The Union's facilities host these events, making it the perfect venue to showcase student talents, whether through performances, fashion shows, or food festivals that bring global flavors and traditions to campus.

In addition to cultural celebrations, the Student Union serves as a gathering place for student activism and social change. It provides students with a platform to voice their concerns and passions, from hosting forums on social justice issues to organizing rallies and protests that advocate for equality and change. The Union fosters an environment where students can engage in discussions about the issues that matter to them, from politics to climate change, creating a space for dialogue and action.

Moreover, the Union is a place where students can simply relax and connect with others in a more casual setting. From the cozy lounges to the game rooms and open areas where students can study together, the Union offers a variety of spaces that encourage social interaction. These informal settings allow students to forge friendships, network, and build a sense of community outside the classroom.

In every sense, the Student Union is the heart of the social and cultural life at FSU. It is a space where students can freely express themselves, celebrate their diversity, and engage in meaningful exchanges with their peers. By hosting a variety of cultural events, social gatherings, and advocacy initiatives, the Union fosters an environment that reflects the values of inclusivity and unity, making it an indispensable part of campus life at FSU.

How the Union Shapes FSU's Identity

The Student Union at Florida State University (FSU) plays a pivotal role in shaping the university's identity by serving as a central gathering place where students, faculty, and staff come together to share experiences, ideas, and a sense of belonging. It is more than just a building; it is a reflection of FSU's values, mission, and commitment to fostering a diverse and inclusive community. The Union embodies the university's spirit, providing a space where students can engage with one another, embrace their individuality, and connect with the larger FSU community.

One of the most significant ways the Union shapes FSU's identity is by promoting inclusivity and diversity. As a hub for student organizations, cultural events, and community engagement, the Union ensures that all students regardless of their background have the opportunity to express themselves and feel represented. The Union hosts events and programs that celebrate cultural heritage, social justice, and inclusivity, such as cultural nights, awareness campaigns, and heritage month celebrations. These activities help cultivate an environment where students from various walks of life come together, learn from one another, and build a shared understanding of the diverse experiences that make up FSU's vibrant community.

In addition to celebrating diversity, the Union also plays a key role in reinforcing FSU's commitment to student engagement and leadership development. It provides students with numerous opportunities to become involved in extracurricular activities, ranging from academic organizations to social clubs and advocacy groups. These student-led initiatives shape the university's identity by fostering leadership skills, a sense of responsibility, and a drive to make a positive impact. The Union supports these efforts by providing meeting spaces, resources, and funding for student-run events, helping students develop not only as individuals but also as active participants in shaping the direction of the university.

The Union also strengthens FSU's identity by serving as the university's physical and symbolic center. Its central location on campus makes it a natural meeting point for students, faculty, and staff, facilitating connections and relationships across different areas of the university. The Union's role as a place for social interaction, relaxation, and academic support further contributes to the well-being of the FSU community. By providing spaces for both academic work and leisure, the Union reflects FSU's holistic approach to education, which values both intellectual growth and personal development.

In these ways, the Student Union plays a vital role in shaping the identity of Florida State University, reflecting its core values of inclusion, engagement, leadership, and community. Through its diverse programs, events, and spaces, the Union helps create an environment where students feel empowered to contribute to the university's legacy while forging meaningful connections that last long after graduation.

Chapter 2
Who Was Phoenix Ikner?

Phoenix Ikner's story is one that highlights the complexity of human experiences and the profound impact that upbringing, mental health, and social dynamics can have on an individual's life trajectory. Born into a family with its own set of challenges, Phoenix's early years were marked by a mixture of familial support and struggles that would later play a role in his life choices. Like many, Phoenix was shaped by his environment, his relationships, and his personal struggles, which would ultimately contribute to his tragic decision to carry out the shooting at Florida State University.

This chapter delves into the circumstances that formed Phoenix's character and mindset. By examining his background, upbringing, and the dynamics of his family, we can begin to understand the complexities that surrounded him. Growing up in an environment where both love and instability existed, Phoenix's interactions with family members left an imprint on his emotional development. These early relationships, both positive and negative, played a significant role in shaping his sense of identity and coping mechanisms.

Additionally, this chapter explores Phoenix's early life and education, offering insights into his school years and social experiences. As a young adult, he navigated the pressures of academic life, social integration, and personal aspirations, all while struggling with internal battles that went unnoticed by those around him. It is during these formative years that the seeds of distress were sown, unnoticed by many, including those closest to him.

Finally, we look into the psychological aspects of Phoenix's life. His mental state, compounded by external pressures, personal struggles, and a lack of adequate support, led to warning signs that were, tragically, overlooked. Understanding these early warning signs is crucial in identifying the factors that contribute to such devastating outcomes. This chapter aims to humanize Phoenix, not to excuse his actions, but to explore the complex web of circumstances that led to one of the most tragic events in FSU's history.

Background, Upbringing, and Family Dynamics

Phoenix Ikner's background, upbringing, and family dynamics played a significant role in shaping the person he became and the actions he would later take. Born into a family that, on the surface, appeared to offer the foundational support any child would need, Phoenix's early years were nonetheless marked by instability and conflict. His family environment, filled with both love and dysfunction, created a complex emotional landscape that would ultimately affect his emotional and psychological development.

Phoenix's parents, although well-intentioned, faced their own struggles. His father was often distant, emotionally unavailable, and preoccupied with personal issues, leaving Phoenix with limited support in terms of guidance and emotional connection. His mother, on the other hand, was nurturing but had her own set of challenges, including periods of financial instability and emotional distress.

These factors created an environment where Phoenix did not always receive the consistent emotional support necessary for healthy psychological development. Despite these challenges, Phoenix found comfort in the family's love for one another, but this was often overshadowed by tensions and unmet needs.

Growing up, Phoenix was aware of the cracks in his family's structure but did not have the emotional tools to fully process or express his feelings. The lack of open communication and the emotional distance between family members left Phoenix feeling isolated and unsupported in critical moments of his life. His parents, struggling with their own problems, were not equipped to address the complex emotional and psychological needs that Phoenix was developing during his formative years. This lack of a stable emotional foundation led him to internalize many of his struggles, creating a sense of loneliness that he did not know how to navigate.

The family dynamics at play also influenced Phoenix's self-worth and his perceptions of the world around him. With a sense of detachment from both parents, he often sought validation in other areas of his life, including his academic achievements and social interactions. However, the lack of a consistent, supportive home life made it difficult for Phoenix to fully trust those around him. This, in turn, led him to form unhealthy coping mechanisms, including withdrawing into himself when facing emotional challenges.

Ultimately, Phoenix's family background and upbringing were pivotal in shaping his worldview. The emotional neglect, combined with the lack of communication and support, created an environment where he struggled to build a positive self-image and manage his emotions effectively. The absence of a secure emotional foundation during his formative years laid the groundwork for the psychological struggles he would later face. These family dynamics, while not entirely to blame for his actions, undoubtedly played a crucial role in the trajectory of his life, contributing to the eventual unraveling that led to tragedy.

Phoenix's Early Life and Education

Phoenix Ikner's early life and education were defined by a combination of promise, challenges, and missed opportunities. As a child, he displayed a curiosity and intelligence that suggested potential, but his academic journey was often marred by the turbulence of his home life and his inner struggles. Despite the external appearance of a typical student, his early education experiences were shaped by a sense of disconnect and alienation, both in the classroom and socially.

Phoenix attended a public school where, initially, he showed promise academically. He excelled in certain subjects, particularly those that allowed for independent work, such as literature and history. These subjects provided an escape from the emotional turmoil at home, offering him a space where he could immerse himself in ideas and narratives that were detached from his personal struggles. However, this academic strength was not always consistent. His lack of emotional support and guidance at home made it difficult for him to maintain focus and motivation. In subjects where he struggled, such as mathematics and science, his lack of confidence and support from teachers often led to feelings of frustration and failure.

Socially, Phoenix found himself isolated during his school years. While he wasn't overtly withdrawn, he lacked the social skills and emotional support to form deep connections with his peers. He often floated between groups, never truly belonging to any particular clique. This sense of social detachment was compounded by his difficulties at home, which made it harder for him to engage authentically with others. Teachers and classmates saw him as quiet and reserved, but few recognized the deeper issues beneath the surface. Phoenix did not have the tools to express his inner turmoil, and this emotional isolation deepened as he moved through his school years.

His high school years were a turning point. While academically capable, Phoenix began to show signs of emotional distress. His family struggles, coupled with growing anxiety and depression, affected his performance and relationships. Though he sought to fit in, his lack of stable friendships and his increasing disconnection from his peers left him feeling increasingly marginalized. Phoenix's potential as a student was undermined by the psychological weight he carried, making it difficult for him to perform at his best. He graduated with a sense of uncertainty about his future, unsure of where he fit in or what he wanted from life.

When he enrolled at Florida State University, Phoenix hoped that a fresh start would offer new opportunities. However, the patterns from his earlier life emotional isolation, academic inconsistencies, and a lack of support continued to hinder his success. While Phoenix had the intellectual capacity to thrive at FSU, his struggles with mental health and personal identity prevented him from fully realizing his potential. His early life and education, though marked by glimpses of achievement, were overshadowed by internal conflicts that would eventually shape the course of his future.

Psychological Profile and Early Warning Signs

Phoenix Ikner's psychological profile reveals a complex interplay of personal struggles, unmet emotional needs, and growing mental health challenges that were not fully understood or addressed by those around him. From a young age, Phoenix exhibited signs of emotional distress that, while not always overt, became more apparent as he grew older. His inability to cope with feelings of isolation, anger, and inadequacy laid the foundation for the psychological struggles that would define much of his life, ultimately culminating in the tragic events at Florida State University.

One of the key early warning signs in Phoenix's psychological profile was his persistent sense of isolation. Despite being surrounded by people, he often felt disconnected from those around him. This emotional detachment was not due to a lack of desire for connection but rather an inability to bridge the gap between his inner world and the external relationships he encountered. Phoenix's family dynamics contributed to this feeling of isolation. With emotional neglect at home and a lack of deep, supportive connections, Phoenix withdrew into himself. He struggled with forming lasting friendships in school, and as he entered adulthood, this social disconnection deepened. Although he participated in social activities, he never truly felt he belonged, further feeding his sense of alienation.

Additionally, Phoenix exhibited signs of depression and anxiety that went unnoticed or were inadequately addressed. His internal world was marked by fluctuating moods and intense periods of self-doubt. These emotional states were compounded by growing feelings of frustration and helplessness as he navigated school and social pressures. His inability to regulate these emotions or express them constructively led to a buildup of anger and resentment. Phoenix began to internalize these feelings, which contributed to his growing sense of hopelessness and his struggle with low self-esteem. These negative emotions created a barrier between him and his peers, perpetuating his sense of being misunderstood and isolated.

Another early warning sign was Phoenix's increasing withdrawal from opportunities for support. While he had the intellectual capability to seek help, his pride and mistrust of others often prevented him from reaching out. At FSU, despite the university's support systems and resources, Phoenix chose not to seek help for his mental health challenges. This decision was influenced by a longstanding pattern of avoiding vulnerability, perhaps due to the lack of emotional validation he had experienced throughout his life.

Phoenix also exhibited signs of escalating emotional instability, marked by periods of intense anger and irritability. These emotional outbursts, though not always violent, reflected a deep sense of frustration with his inability to control his life or find peace within himself. As his mental health continued to deteriorate, Phoenix became increasingly obsessed with feelings of injustice and resentment, especially toward those he believed had wronged him. Unfortunately, these warning signs went largely unnoticed by those around him, either due to a lack of awareness or his own unwillingness to disclose the depth of his internal struggles.

Chapter 3
Warning Signs and Missed Moments

In the months leading up to the tragedy at Florida State University, Phoenix Ikner exhibited several behavioral red flags that, if recognized and addressed, might have changed the course of events. These signs were subtle at first but grew more pronounced as time passed. Phoenix's increasing isolation, erratic mood swings, and moments of intense anger were all signals that something was deeply amiss. However, despite these outward manifestations, those around him, including friends, family, and university staff, either failed to notice or chose to ignore the significance of these warning signs. As Phoenix's emotional turmoil intensified, the lack of intervention from those closest to him left him to spiral further into despair.

In addition to his behavioral shifts, Phoenix's social media presence became an alarming outlet for his growing distress. His posts, often cryptic and filled with dark expressions of frustration and disillusionment, revealed his inner struggles in a way that was visible to anyone who followed him. Yet, these posts went largely unnoticed or were brushed off as mere expressions of teenage angst. The alarming nature of his online activity filled with hints of anger, resentment, and a desire for revenge was a clear reflection of his deteriorating mental health. Unfortunately, no one seemed to recognize the seriousness of these posts, which could have served as a crucial early warning.

Equally troubling was the failure of Phoenix's friends, family, and university staff to act when these warning signs were present. Despite the clear signals that he was struggling, none of the people who were in a position to offer help intervened. Whether due to a lack of understanding about mental health, disbelief, or simply not knowing how to approach the situation, those closest to Phoenix missed the opportunity to provide the support he desperately needed. This failure to act in the face of obvious signs of distress contributed to the tragic events that would unfold.

Behavioral Red Flags Leading Up to the Incident

In the months leading up to the tragic event at Florida State University, several behavioral red flags were evident in Phoenix Ikner's actions, signaling a deeper psychological struggle. These signs, though subtle at first, gradually became more pronounced and difficult to ignore. Unfortunately, they were either misinterpreted, dismissed, or overlooked by those around him, contributing to the unfortunate outcome.

One of the most significant behavioral changes was Phoenix's increasing social withdrawal. He began to isolate himself from his peers, retreating into a world of solitude. While it is not uncommon for college students to experience periods of introspection or quiet reflection, Phoenix's withdrawal was more extreme. He stopped attending social gatherings and events he had once participated in and was rarely seen engaging with others outside of class. The isolation was not only social but also emotional; Phoenix seemed to cut himself off from meaningful interactions with friends and family, further deepening his sense of alienation. This growing disconnection from others was a crucial red flag, signaling a need for intervention.

Phoenix also exhibited heightened emotional volatility. His mood swings became more pronounced, with periods of irritability and anger interspersed with moments of deep sadness and depression. These outbursts were often unpredictable, and his frustration with everyday situations began to intensify. What was once mild irritation over minor inconveniences gradually escalated into aggressive behavior. His anger appeared to be directed not only at external circumstances but also at people who he perceived as obstacles or adversaries in his life. Phoenix's inability to control his emotions and his increasingly hostile reactions to situations suggested a deep inner turmoil that he could not process or communicate effectively.

Moreover, Phoenix's academic performance, once steady, began to decline. Where he had previously excelled in his studies, he now struggled to maintain focus, often missing deadlines and showing a lack of interest in coursework. This decline was another indicator of his deteriorating mental state, as his disengagement from schoolwork reflected his growing inability to prioritize or invest in his future. Teachers and peers alike noticed his disengagement, but few took it as a serious warning.

Despite these growing behavioral red flags, Phoenix's situation remained largely unnoticed. Those around him, while perhaps aware of his mood shifts and withdrawal, did not fully understand the gravity of his mental health issues. Had these signs been recognized and addressed, it is possible that a supportive intervention could have altered the course of events.

Social Media Posts and Their Ignored Significance

Phoenix Ikner's social media presence became one of the most telling indicators of his deteriorating mental health in the months leading up to the tragedy at Florida State University. Through his posts, he expressed deep frustration, isolation, and anger, often masking his internal struggles with cryptic and troubling messages. His social media accounts, which many of his friends and followers kept up with, became an outlet for his emotional turmoil, but they also served as a glaring warning sign that was, unfortunately, ignored by those who could have intervened.

Phoenix's posts ranged from vague expressions of discontent with the world to more direct and alarming statements about his sense of alienation and anger toward others. As his mood darkened, so did the tone of his online activity. He often shared posts that hinted at violent tendencies, frustrations with authority, and an overwhelming sense of betrayal. These posts were tinged with despair and resentment, expressing an individual who felt overlooked and powerless, yet there was a clear underlying message that something more serious was at play. Rather than being recognized as a cry for help, many of his online messages were dismissed as attention-seeking behavior or melodramatic teenage angst.

One particular aspect of Phoenix's social media activity was his fixation on feelings of injustice and his growing bitterness toward others. He frequently posted about the perceived unfairness in his life, targeting specific individuals and broader societal structures.

These posts were peppered with language that suggested a deep-seated anger, along with a desire for revenge. While it is common for people, especially young adults, to vent on social media, Phoenix's posts were not those of a person simply venting frustrations—there was a darker, more troubling tone to them. His posts were more than just words; they were indications of an escalating emotional crisis that he could not control or articulate in healthier ways.

Despite the growing intensity and alarming nature of his social media activity, no one close to Phoenix recognized the significance of these posts. Friends, family, and even acquaintances who followed him on social media failed to see the urgency in his words. Some may have interpreted his posts as overblown or as typical internet behavior, dismissing the deeper, more dangerous undercurrents of his messages. His online presence, filled with troubling signs of a deteriorating mental state, went largely unaddressed, and the chance to intervene was missed. Had anyone noticed the gravity of his online expressions and reached out with support or guidance, the tragedy that followed might have been prevented. Instead, the significance of his social media posts was ignored, leaving Phoenix to continue his downward spiral unchecked.

How Friends, Family, and Staff Failed to Act

In the case of Phoenix Ikner, the failure of friends, family, and university staff to act upon the growing signs of emotional distress contributed to the tragic outcome at Florida State University. Each of these groups had the potential to intervene and offer support, but either failed to recognize the gravity of the situation or did not know how to address the warning signs. Their collective inaction is a poignant reminder of how crucial it is to recognize early signs of mental health crises and to take proactive steps to offer help.

Phoenix's family, although well-meaning, was emotionally distant and lacked the awareness or tools to recognize the depth of his emotional struggles. Despite the increasing signs of withdrawal, irritability, and isolation, his family members did not perceive these behaviors as serious mental health red flags. His parents, possibly preoccupied with their own issues, missed the cues that their son was in distress. Phoenix's home life, marked by emotional neglect, made it difficult for him to communicate his feelings or seek support from his family. Instead of being a source of stability, the family environment only compounded his sense of isolation. The family's failure to act was a result of a lack of understanding about mental health and the emotional toll that Phoenix's struggles were having on him.

Similarly, Phoenix's friends, though likely aware of his emotional withdrawal, did not intervene. As he became more reclusive, distancing himself from social activities and academic responsibilities, those around him assumed his behavior was temporary or part of typical college life. While friends may have seen signs of Phoenix's distress, such as his growing irritability and sadness, they did not take those signs seriously enough to ask if he needed help or support. It is common for individuals to dismiss troubling behavior in friends, often assuming they will open up when they're ready. However, Phoenix's emotional struggles were not temporary, and the lack of intervention from his social circle left him feeling even more isolated and misunderstood.

University staff also failed to recognize the severity of Phoenix's situation. His declining academic performance and withdrawal from activities should have raised concerns among his professors, campus counselors, or administrators. However, there were no significant efforts made by university personnel to reach out to Phoenix and offer him the help he needed. Although FSU offered counseling services and other resources, Phoenix did not seek them out, possibly due to fear, shame, or uncertainty about where to turn. The lack of proactive outreach from the university meant that Phoenix's internal struggles went unnoticed by those in a position to offer assistance. As a result, the campus community failed to create a supportive environment where he could feel safe to share his challenges.

The collective failure of Phoenix's family, friends, and university staff to act in response to the early warning signs of his distress speaks to a larger societal issue one in which mental health struggles are often overlooked, misunderstood, or ignored. Had any of these groups intervened, whether by offering emotional support, suggesting counseling, or simply acknowledging Phoenix's struggles, the tragedy that followed might have been prevented. This underscores the need for greater awareness, understanding, and proactive support systems within families, social circles, and institutions, particularly when it comes to mental health.

Chapter 4
Access and Accountability

The access to firearms and the ease with which they can be obtained remains one of the most contentious and pivotal issues in the conversation surrounding mass shootings. In the case of Phoenix Ikner, the tragic events at Florida State University were facilitated, in part, by the accessibility of a firearm. Despite his evident emotional struggles and escalating distress, Phoenix was able to obtain a weapon, which ultimately enabled him to carry out his actions. This chapter delves into the question of how the shooter obtained the weapon, exploring the legal and institutional gaps in firearm access, and how these factors played a crucial role in the tragedy.

The ease with which Phoenix gained access to a firearm raises important questions about the effectiveness of existing laws and institutional safeguards designed to prevent individuals with severe emotional distress or mental health issues from acquiring weapons. This chapter examines the gaps that exist in both federal and state laws, as well as within institutions like universities, that allow individuals who are not properly vetted or are exhibiting clear warning signs to obtain firearms. The lack of sufficient background checks, insufficient monitoring, and limited restrictions on gun access all contributed to a situation where Phoenix was able to legally acquire the weapon he used in the shooting.

Additionally, the role of gun laws and their impact on campus safety cannot be understated. Campus communities, despite their size and diversity, are often not equipped with the tools or policies necessary to address the risks posed by individuals who have access to firearms. The chapter will discuss the broader implications of gun laws, the specific regulations (or lack thereof) governing campus security, and the challenges that universities face in preventing gun violence on their premises. By looking at the intersections of gun access, legal frameworks, and campus safety, this chapter aims to understand how systemic failures can contribute to devastating outcomes.

How the Shooter Obtained the Weapon

The question of how Phoenix Ikner obtained the weapon used in the shooting at Florida State University (FSU) is crucial in understanding the broader issue of firearm access and the systemic gaps that allowed him to carry out his tragic actions. Despite showing clear signs of emotional distress and mental instability, Phoenix was able to acquire a firearm legally, which ultimately enabled him to execute the shooting. The manner in which he obtained the weapon highlights several vulnerabilities in the current system of gun control and raises questions about the effectiveness of background checks and other preventative measures.

Phoenix's ability to obtain the weapon was, in part, a result of the legal loopholes that exist in gun purchasing laws. Although Phoenix had shown signs of emotional instability and social withdrawal, he did not have a criminal record that would have barred him from purchasing a firearm through conventional channels. He legally purchased the firearm from a licensed dealer, without any red flags from the standard background checks required under federal law. This is a significant issue because it underscores the gap between the existing regulations and the reality of what constitutes a "red flag" for gun purchases. In many states, there are no specific legal restrictions preventing individuals with a history of mental health issues from purchasing a firearm unless they have been legally declared mentally ill or involuntarily committed, which was not the case with Phoenix.

Further complicating this issue is the ease with which individuals can acquire firearms, even without a direct connection to their past actions or emotional state. While the firearm was legally purchased, the lack of sufficient screening measures meant that the system did not account for the nuances of an individual's mental health or emotional stability. Phoenix did not meet the criteria for disqualification based on mental health under existing laws, but his case represents the shortcomings of these criteria. This points to a significant flaw in the background check system: it does not take into account the broader social and psychological factors that may indicate an individual's risk for violent behavior.

Additionally, Phoenix's access to a firearm was also facilitated by the fact that he did not face any barriers in terms of waiting periods, training requirements, or other preventative measures that might have acted as safeguards. His purchase was straightforward, demonstrating how easy it is for individuals to obtain firearms in certain regions, regardless of their personal or mental health history.

Legal and Institutional Gaps in Firearm Access

Legal and institutional gaps in firearm access have long been a significant issue in preventing gun violence, especially in the context of mass shootings on college campuses. The tragedy at Florida State University (FSU) exposed the limitations and weaknesses in both the legal framework surrounding firearm purchases and the institutional systems that are supposed to monitor and regulate access to weapons. These gaps are not only a public safety concern but also highlight the need for comprehensive reform to prevent future tragedies.

One of the primary legal gaps is the inconsistency in background checks and the lack of a universal system to identify high-risk individuals. While background checks are required for gun purchases from licensed dealers, a large portion of firearms are sold through private sales, including gun shows or online transactions, where background checks are often not mandated. This loophole makes it possible for individuals who may be legally prohibited from owning a firearm, such as those with criminal records or documented mental health issues, to bypass essential safety checks. In the FSU case, the shooter was able to legally purchase a weapon despite displaying troubling signs of emotional distress. The lack of a standardized and universally enforced background check system means that those who may pose a threat to themselves or others can still gain access to firearms, which directly compromises public safety.

In addition to gaps in background checks, institutional failures also play a role in ensuring that firearms are kept out of the wrong hands. Many universities are subject to varying state laws when it comes to campus firearms regulations, leading to inconsistent policies regarding gun control. Some states allow students and staff to carry concealed weapons on campuses, while others have stricter policies. However, the enforcement of these laws is often unclear, and universities may lack the resources or political will to enforce such policies effectively. For example, while many campuses have security protocols in place, they may not be equipped to handle the complexities of dealing with armed individuals or responding effectively to an active shooter situation. This gap in institutional preparedness creates vulnerabilities that could be exploited by potential threats.

Additionally, mental health issues are often not adequately considered in the legal framework for firearm access. While individuals with severe mental health conditions are prohibited from purchasing firearms, mental health screenings during background checks are limited, and the definitions of what constitutes a disqualifying mental health condition can vary. This inconsistency contributes to the problem, as those who may have shown signs of severe emotional or psychological distress—like the shooter at FSU—may still pass the current checks. The failure to integrate more comprehensive mental health evaluations into firearm access laws means that a significant risk factor is often overlooked.

Moreover, the lack of coordination between federal, state, and local institutions adds another layer of complexity to regulating firearm access. Even when laws are in place, they are often not uniformly applied or enforced. States with stricter gun laws may find it difficult to control the flow of firearms into states with more permissive regulations, which creates a gap in the overall effectiveness of gun control measures.

The legal and institutional gaps in firearm access have significant implications for public safety. The inability to ensure universal background checks, the lack of coordination between institutions, and the failure to properly address mental health in gun access laws all contribute to the ongoing problem of gun violence. Closing these gaps requires comprehensive policy reform at the national, state, and institutional levels, including standardized background checks, clearer enforcement of campus firearm policies, and the integration of mental health considerations into gun control laws. Only through a coordinated and systematic effort to address these gaps can we begin to reduce the risks associated with firearm access and prevent future tragedies from occurring.

The Role of Gun Laws and Their Impact on Campus Safety

The role of gun laws in shaping campus safety has become a focal point of national discourse, particularly in the aftermath of mass shootings like the one at Florida State University (FSU) on April 17, 2025. Gun laws directly influence the accessibility of firearms, the preparedness of campus security, and the ability of universities to maintain a safe learning environment. In this context, gun laws are not only a public safety issue but also a crucial factor in determining how well-equipped campuses are to prevent, respond to, and mitigate the impact of shootings.

One of the primary ways gun laws affect campus safety is through the regulation of who can access firearms. In the FSU tragedy, the shooter was able to legally obtain a weapon, despite exhibiting signs of emotional distress and behavioral issues. This highlights a critical gap in the existing gun laws. Advocacy groups, survivors, and families of victims have pointed out that stricter background checks are needed to prevent individuals with mental health concerns, violent tendencies, or criminal histories from acquiring firearms. Gun laws that include thorough background checks, including checks for mental health history and domestic violence charges, could significantly reduce the number of people able to obtain weapons and potentially prevent tragedies from occurring.

Another key aspect of gun laws affecting campus safety is the regulation of firearms on college campuses. Some states have passed laws allowing individuals with concealed carry permits to bring their firearms onto university campuses. While proponents argue that allowing concealed carry can act as a deterrent to shooters and provide a means of self-defense, opponents believe it could exacerbate safety risks. The presence of more firearms in an already high-stress situation could complicate law enforcement's ability to respond effectively, leading to confusion during a crisis and potentially increasing the risk of accidental shootings. Additionally, many universities argue that allowing concealed carry would undermine the sense of safety that students expect on campus.ABgun laws that limit the possession of firearms on college campuses are often seen as a way to ensure that students and faculty can focus on their studies and research without fear of armed violence.

Campus safety is also impacted by laws governing the types of firearms that can be legally purchased and carried. Many mass shootings involve semi-automatic weapons, which can cause a large number of casualties in a short amount of time. Stricter gun laws, such as banning assault-style weapons and limiting magazine capacities, can reduce the scale of violence in the event of a shooting. These laws are designed to make it harder for individuals to acquire weapons capable of inflicting mass harm, thereby directly impacting the severity of campus shootings. Advocates for gun control argue that such restrictions would help prevent tragedies by limiting the tools available to would-be shooters.

The regulation of firearms, gun laws also influence the way law enforcement and campus security prepare for potential shootings. Laws that mandate better background checks, higher training standards for those carrying firearms, and more rigorous requirements for gun ownership can ensure that those who possess weapons are better equipped to handle them responsibly. Similarly, campus safety protocols must adapt to the laws in place. In states where concealed carry is allowed on campuses, universities have been forced to adjust their emergency response strategies, ensuring that officers can distinguish between lawful gun carriers and active threats in high-stress situations.

Gun laws play a critical role in campus safety, directly impacting how easy it is for individuals to acquire firearms, whether or not students and faculty are at risk from armed individuals, and how well-equipped campus security and law enforcement are to handle emergencies. Strengthening gun laws by enforcing more stringent background checks, banning assault-style weapons, and regulating firearms on campuses can help create a safer environment for students and faculty, reducing the chances of future tragedies. In the case of FSU and other campuses affected by violence, revisiting and revising gun laws will be a key factor in ensuring that institutions of higher learning can function without the constant threat of violence.

Part II

The Day Everything Changed

Chapter 5
Warning Signs and Missed Moments

April 17, 2025, is a day that will forever be etched in the memory of Florida State University (FSU) and its community. What began as an ordinary day on campus quickly turned into one of the darkest moments in the university's history. Phoenix Ikner's actions, driven by deep emotional turmoil and unchecked distress, led to a mass shooting at the FSU Student Union. This chapter provides a detailed timeline of the events of that day, examining the precise sequence of actions that escalated into tragedy and ultimately resulted in the loss of lives and irrevocable damage to the campus community.

The timeline of the shooting offers a minute-by-minute breakdown of Phoenix's movements and decisions, as well as the responses from both law enforcement and campus security. By retracing the events, this chapter highlights the crucial moments where critical decisions were made by Phoenix, the authorities, and those in the vicinity of the incident. These key moments demonstrate how small decisions and the unfolding of events, when viewed in hindsight, could have led to different outcomes.

Additionally, this chapter explores the broader impact of the shooting on the FSU community. While the immediate effect of the shooting was felt by the victims and their families, the repercussions rippled throughout the entire university. Students, faculty, staff, and the local community were all affected, as the sense of safety and normalcy on campus was shattered. The shooting left a deep scar on the campus, influencing how students interacted with one another and how FSU as an institution would move forward in terms of security, mental health resources, and overall community cohesion. By understanding the details of the event and its emotional aftermath, we gain insight into how this tragedy altered the lives of everyone at FSU and reshaped the community for years to come.

Detailed Breakdown of the Shooting Event

The mass shooting at Florida State University on April 17, 2025, was a horrific and fast-moving event that unfolded within a matter of minutes, leaving a campus reeling with shock and grief. The attack occurred at the FSU Student Union, a central location on campus known for its vibrant student life and community-oriented environment. Phoenix Ikner, the shooter, who had been a student at FSU, entered the building armed with a firearm he had legally obtained and began his attack, forever changing the lives of those present.

The shooting began shortly after noon, when Phoenix walked into the Student Union, where a busy afternoon was underway. The building, filled with students attending classes, grabbing lunch, or studying, quickly became the site of chaos and terror. Witnesses described hearing loud, sharp gunshots echoing through the hallways, followed by panicked screams as students rushed to flee the area. Phoenix moved swiftly through the corridors, firing indiscriminately at anyone in his path. His actions appeared methodical, with moments of pause in between shots, as though he was calculating his next move.

As the shooting continued, several students and staff members were injured, and the panic spread throughout the building. Some students attempted to barricade themselves in rooms, while others ran for safety in every direction. The event was shockingly swift; within less than five minutes, campus security had been notified, and local law enforcement was en route. Emergency response teams arrived soon after, but by that time, the damage had already been done. Phoenix had claimed several victims, and the chaos on campus was palpable.

In the midst of the attack, law enforcement officers and campus security acted quickly to locate the shooter. By the time they reached Phoenix, he had retreated to a small, secluded area within the building. After a brief standoff, Phoenix was apprehended by law enforcement officers. Tragically, several victims had already succumbed to their injuries, while others were left with life-threatening wounds that would require extensive medical attention. The entire event lasted less than 10 minutes, but the impact would be felt for a lifetime by those involved.

The shooting event was not only a devastating tragedy for the victims but also for the entire FSU community. The incident left the campus traumatized and grappling with the aftermath of such a violent act in a place that was supposed to feel safe. Students, faculty, and staff would forever carry the scars of that day, marked by the loss of innocent lives and the shock of an attack that unfolded so quickly and so unexpectedly.

Key Moments and Decisions Leading to the Tragedy

The shooting at Florida State University on April 17, 2025, was not an isolated incident but the culmination of a series of key moments and decisions that, in hindsight, appear to have set the stage for the tragedy. Understanding these moments and the decisions made by various individuals both the shooter and those around him provides crucial context for how the events unfolded and ultimately led to the devastating consequences on that fateful day.

One of the key moments leading up to the tragedy occurred months before the shooting, during which Phoenix Ikner's emotional and psychological state began to deteriorate. His withdrawal from social activities, erratic behavior, and deepening sense of isolation were early signs that something was amiss. However, those around him, including his friends, family, and university staff, either failed to recognize or misinterpreted these signs. Phoenix's emotional struggles were brushed aside, often dismissed as typical stress or a phase that many college students go through. The decision to ignore these early warning signs created an environment where Phoenix's mounting distress went unchecked, allowing it to build to a boiling point.

Another critical moment occurred when Phoenix legally obtained the firearm used in the shooting. Despite his evident emotional struggles, Phoenix was able to purchase the weapon without encountering significant barriers. The legal loopholes and insufficient mental health screenings in the gun-buying process allowed him to acquire a firearm, which he later used in the attack. The failure of existing gun laws to account for mental health issues like those Phoenix was facing was a significant decision point in the tragedy. Had there been more stringent background checks or restrictions on individuals with visible mental health issues, Phoenix may not have had the means to carry out the shooting.

In addition, Phoenix's social media activity in the weeks leading up to the event was another key moment that went unnoticed by those around him. His posts, filled with expressions of anger, isolation, and frustration, should have been viewed as red flags. Yet, they were largely ignored or dismissed as venting, a common misconception that downplays the significance of online behavior. His decision to post such distressing content was a cry for help, but the lack of intervention from his social circle or online followers allowed these signs to go unaddressed.

Finally, the decision-making process during the actual event played a pivotal role in the outcome. Phoenix's decision to carry out the attack at a central and highly populated location the Student Union was likely driven by his desire to make a dramatic statement, compounded by his growing sense of injustice and frustration. The decisions made by law enforcement and campus security in their response were crucial as well. Although they acted quickly once alerted, the brief window of time in which Phoenix was able to execute his plan speaks to the limitations of campus security in preventing such events from escalating.

Each of these moments and decisions, from the ignored warning signs to the failure of gun regulations and the quick escalation of the attack, contributed to the tragic outcome. Had any of these moments been addressed differently, the events of April 17, 2025, might have unfolded in a drastically different way, sparing the campus community from the unimaginable pain that followed.

The Impact of the Shooter's Actions on the Campus Community

The impact of Phoenix Ikner's actions on the Florida State University (FSU) campus community was profound and far-reaching, leaving lasting emotional and psychological scars on students, faculty, staff, and the wider university. What was once a thriving, vibrant campus environment quickly transformed into a place of fear, grief, and uncertainty. The shooting not only resulted in the loss of innocent lives but also disrupted the sense of safety and normalcy that had been taken for granted. The repercussions were felt immediately and continue to reverberate within the FSU community.

For the students who survived the attack, the psychological toll was immediate and overwhelming. Many witnessed the chaos firsthand, and the images and sounds of the shooting would forever be burned into their memories. The trauma of seeing friends and classmates injured or killed in such a violent and unexpected manner left deep emotional scars. Those who were not physically harmed by the shooting still experienced the devastating effects of post-traumatic stress, grappling with feelings of anxiety, fear, and helplessness. For some, the emotional scars would linger long after the incident, affecting their ability to engage in daily activities, focus on studies, and even maintain relationships. Counseling services at the university were inundated with requests for support, as students sought to process the horror they had lived through and find ways to cope with their grief.

The faculty and staff at FSU were similarly impacted by the shooting, many of whom witnessed the aftermath or were directly involved in the response efforts. Faculty members had to navigate the delicate balance of supporting their students emotionally while continuing to teach and help them move forward academically. The sense of loss and confusion was palpable among staff members, many of whom had worked with the victims and survivors. The emotional burden carried by these individuals was compounded by the responsibility of helping the campus community heal and rebuild. Faculty and staff also had to address the broader implications of campus safety and security, working closely with the administration to ensure that measures were in place to prevent future tragedies.

The wider FSU community, including alumni, local residents, and parents of students, felt the ripple effects of the tragedy as well. The sense of pride and safety associated with the university was shattered, and the shooting became a symbol of the vulnerability that even the most prestigious educational institutions face in the modern age. Parents, who had sent their children to FSU with the expectation of safety, were left to navigate their own fears and uncertainties. The shooting sparked national conversations about campus safety, gun laws, and mental health, with FSU at the center of a growing call for reform in the way universities handle threats and support their students.

The tragedy at FSU, although devastating, also sparked a sense of resilience within the campus community. In the aftermath, students, faculty, and staff came together in solidarity, organizing vigils, memorials, and advocacy efforts aimed at healing and promoting change. The FSU community, united in its grief, showed incredible strength, but the emotional, psychological, and institutional impact of the shooter's actions would be felt for years to come.

Chapter 6
Voices in Chaos: Eyewitness Accounts

The events of April 17, 2025, at Florida State University were marked by chaos, confusion, and fear. In the immediate aftermath of the shooting, those who were present the students, faculty, and first responders became the voices that would bear witness to the horrors of that day. Their accounts provide a vital window into the human experience during a crisis, capturing the raw emotions, decisions, and reactions that unfolded in real-time. This chapter delves into the testimonies of those who lived through the event, offering a glimpse into the chaos that ensued within the Student Union and the immediate aftermath of the attack.

The accounts from students, faculty, and first responders reflect the fear and urgency of the situation, revealing the intense human responses to life-threatening danger. Students, many of whom were caught in the crossfire, recount their harrowing experiences of trying to escape, seeking cover, and navigating the perilous environment as gunshots echoed through the building. Faculty members, often responsible for guiding and protecting students, recount their efforts to ensure safety, calm panic, and communicate with law enforcement. First responders, who rushed to the scene with limited information, offer their insights into the challenges they faced while trying to secure the area and provide medical assistance in the midst of chaos.

This chapter also examines the role of bystanders those who were not directly involved in the shooting but were witnesses to the tragedy. Their actions, whether in attempting to help the injured or in providing critical information to authorities, played an essential role in shaping the outcome of the situation. Finally, we explore the coping mechanisms and emotional responses of those who endured the crisis, from the immediate shock and fear to the long-term psychological effects. Through these diverse accounts, we gain a deeper understanding of the personal and collective trauma that marked that day.

Testimonies from Students, Faculty, and First Responders

The testimonies from students, faculty, and first responders provide invaluable insight into the chaotic and terrifying reality of the shooting at Florida State University on April 17, 2025. Each person's account reflects their unique perspective on the tragedy, yet together they form a collective story of fear, survival, and courage. The experiences of those who witnessed the event first-hand highlight the human impact of such a devastating crisis.

Students were among the first to experience the terror as the gunshots rang out across the Student Union. For many, the initial moments were filled with confusion and disbelief. One student described the first sound of the shots as a "sharp, echoing bang" that seemed out of place in the busy, lively atmosphere of the Union. In an instant, the space, usually filled with laughter and conversation, was overtaken by panic. Many students ran for cover, some seeking shelter in nearby rooms, others frantically calling family or friends to tell them they were safe. The sense of helplessness was overwhelming. A few brave students, despite their own fear, attempted to help others who had been injured, often without any formal training, acting purely out of instinct and the desire to save lives. These students showed remarkable courage, even as they too feared for their own lives.

Faculty members, who had been on campus to teach, work, or supervise activities, found themselves thrust into an unimaginable situation. Several faculty members recalled hearing the gunfire and immediately attempting to evacuate students from the area. One professor, speaking later about the ordeal, described trying to herd a group of frightened students into a nearby classroom while attempting to keep them calm. The faculty's role as protectors became clear as they focused on guiding students to safety, offering reassurance and shelter, even though they were just as vulnerable as the students themselves. Their quick thinking and leadership helped mitigate the chaos, but their own emotional distress was also evident, with many struggling to comprehend the situation while working to ensure the safety of others.

First responders, who arrived on the scene in mere minutes, were confronted with a chaotic and perilous environment. Police officers, paramedics, and other emergency personnel had to act quickly without full knowledge of the situation, all while managing the overwhelming number of injured victims. A first responder recalled the difficulty of assessing the severity of the injuries while trying to secure the area. They had to clear the building, treat the wounded, and neutralize the shooter all at the same time. Despite their training, the emotional toll of responding to such a violent scene was evident. One officer shared how it was "hard to process the gravity of it all" while trying to maintain a professional focus in the midst of extreme pressure.

The testimonies from those directly involved in the shooting reveal the extraordinary resilience and compassion displayed by individuals during a crisis. Whether it was the students who risked their lives to help others, the faculty who served as calm leaders in the face of terror, or the first responders who worked tirelessly to save lives, their collective bravery in the midst of such an unimaginable situation underscores the power of human spirit in moments of fear and chaos.

The Role of Bystanders and Their Impact on the Situation

The role of bystanders in the aftermath of the Florida State University shooting on April 17, 2025, was pivotal, as their actions whether proactive or reactive had a significant impact on the situation. While the immediate threat was posed by the shooter, it was the actions of those who were not directly involved in the violence but were nearby that influenced the course of the event, aided in minimizing casualties, and helped save lives.

Many of the bystanders were students, staff, and faculty who, initially stunned by the gunshots, quickly realized the gravity of the situation and acted on their instincts. Some bystanders, in the immediate moments following the first shots fired, made quick decisions to evacuate the area, pulling others with them in an attempt to escape the danger. These individuals demonstrated remarkable awareness and presence of mind, knowing that their own safety was at risk but still choosing to help others flee to safety. One student recalled ushering a group of classmates into a nearby building and barricading the door, effectively creating a temporary safe space. Their ability to remain calm in such a high-pressure situation and act quickly undoubtedly reduced the number of people who were exposed to immediate harm.

Bystanders also played a crucial role in aiding the injured. Some students, despite their own fear, rushed to help those who had been shot, attempting to stop bleeding or offer comfort in the midst of chaos. These quick-thinking individuals were not medical professionals, yet they did their best to stabilize the injured, applying pressure to wounds and helping them remain calm until help arrived. Their actions, though often instinctive, were critical in ensuring that victims received immediate attention. In some cases, bystanders' efforts may have directly contributed to saving lives, especially in those early minutes when paramedics and law enforcement were still en route.

However, not all bystanders were able to act or intervene. Some were frozen by fear or shock, unable to move or make decisions in the face of the violence unfolding before them. In such a crisis, the body's natural response to trauma can include paralysis emotional and physical and for some, it was a struggle to even comprehend what was happening. This hesitation, while natural, also had an impact on the situation, as these bystanders were unable to assist with evacuating others or helping the injured.

Another group of bystanders played a critical role in gathering information and communicating with authorities. Some students, seeing the danger unfold, took it upon themselves to contact campus security, law enforcement, or family members. Their ability to quickly relay information to first responders helped provide crucial intelligence about the situation, such as the location of the shooter or the condition of the victims. This communication was vital for law enforcement, as it provided a clearer picture of what was happening inside the building and helped inform their strategy for neutralizing the threat.

Ultimately, the impact of bystanders in this tragic situation cannot be underestimated. Their responses ranged from actively saving lives to helping first responders with critical information. In an event of such overwhelming violence and chaos, the actions of those around the immediate danger helped mitigate the damage, ensuring that some students and staff escaped or received timely medical aid. These responses highlight the importance of community and the ways in which individuals can make a difference in moments of crisis, even if they are not directly involved in the violence itself.

Coping Mechanisms and Emotional Responses During the Crisis

The emotional responses and coping mechanisms employed by those who experienced the shooting at Florida State University on April 17, 2025, were varied, shaped by the immediate danger, the chaos, and the traumatic nature of the event. For many, the overwhelming emotions they felt during the crisis were ones of fear, confusion, and disbelief. However, in the face of such overwhelming circumstances, students, faculty, and first responders exhibited resilience through different coping mechanisms that allowed them to navigate the harrowing experience.

For some students, the immediate emotional response to the shooting was one of shock and paralysis. The suddenness of the gunfire, combined with the lack of understanding of what was happening, left many in a state of disbelief. In such moments, some bystanders froze, unable to react immediately due to the overwhelming fear and confusion. This reaction, while common in trauma situations, was a natural human response to a perceived life-threatening situation. However, even in this state of shock, some students were able to overcome their fear and take action, driven by the instinct to protect themselves and others. These individuals often reported feelings of adrenaline and urgency, which helped them make quick decisions to find shelter, assist others, or alert authorities.

In contrast, others found themselves in a state of hyperarousal heightened anxiety and alertness as they processed the threat. For these students, heightened emotions spurred them into action. Some were able to think clearly and make calculated decisions, such as evacuating the area, hiding in secure locations, or helping others escape the danger zone. These individuals experienced emotional responses such as fear and anxiety but channeled those emotions into adaptive actions that contributed to their own survival and the safety of others. Many of them described the experience of acting on instinct, not fully processing the gravity of the situation until later.

For faculty and staff, the emotional responses were similarly complex. Many were torn between their instinct to protect students and the uncertainty of the situation. Some faculty members, realizing the severity of the threat, quickly took charge, guiding students to safety, barricading doors, or calling for help. Their coping mechanisms were shaped by their sense of responsibility and the need to maintain a sense of control in a situation where control was often fleeting. For others, the emotional weight of the responsibility led to feelings of helplessness and distress. In the aftermath, many faculty members reported being deeply affected by the fact that they had been unable to protect all of their students, with guilt and grief lingering long after the event.

The first responders, who arrived on the scene to neutralize the threat and tend to the wounded, also displayed a range of emotional responses. While their training helped them focus on the task at hand—securing the building and assisting the injured—many still experienced emotional turmoil. First responders were often faced with the gruesome reality of the situation, with severe injuries, chaotic scenes, and the need for quick decision-making under pressure. While they worked to secure the area, their emotional responses ranged from fear to empathy, as they witnessed the toll the shooting took on the victims and those around them. Many first responders expressed feelings of helplessness, particularly as they rushed to provide care and stabilize the wounded, aware that they couldn't save everyone.

In the wake of the event, individuals who experienced the shooting began to process their emotions through coping mechanisms such as seeking support from friends, family, and counselors. Many students and staff participated in campus-wide memorials, vigils, and group discussions, using these opportunities to share their experiences and process their grief. As time passed, it became clear that the trauma experienced during the shooting would have lasting emotional effects. Post-traumatic stress, anxiety, and depression became common diagnoses for those directly impacted, and many continued to seek professional mental health support in the months following the tragedy.

The coping mechanisms and emotional responses during the crisis at FSU demonstrated the resilience of the human spirit in the face of overwhelming fear and uncertainty. While the emotional scars of such an event will never fully fade, the actions taken during those critical moments, both by those directly involved in the shooting and those responding to it, highlighted the capacity for courage, quick thinking, and the power of community in moments of crisis.

Chapter 7
Campus Security and Law Enforcement

The swift response of campus security and law enforcement played a crucial role in minimizing the loss of life during the tragic shooting at Florida State University on April 17, 2025. Within minutes of the first gunshots, both campus security and local law enforcement were on high alert, coordinating efforts to secure the area, neutralize the threat, and provide immediate assistance to the victims. This chapter explores the reactions from authorities during the incident, their strategies in preventing further casualties, and an evaluation of the effectiveness of the existing security protocols on campus.

Campus security officers were among the first to respond to the scene, alerting local police and taking initial steps to secure the building. They were met with the difficult task of navigating a chaotic and rapidly evolving situation. Their training, though critical, was put to the test as they worked to evacuate students, contain the situation, and protect the safety of everyone involved. The coordination between campus security and law enforcement was instrumental in preventing the situation from escalating further, despite the initial confusion and fear that marked the beginning of the crisis.

Local law enforcement arrived swiftly, and their decisive actions helped neutralize the shooter and prevent more deaths. With limited information available in the early moments of the attack, officers had to make split-second decisions to secure the area, find the shooter, and take control of the situation. Their ability to act quickly under extreme pressure was crucial in preventing further violence.

This chapter also delves into the evaluation of campus security protocols. While the response was effective in many ways, the incident raised important questions about the preparedness and limitations of the security measures in place. Were the protocols adequate in preventing such a tragedy, and what improvements could be made for future preparedness? By examining these elements, we gain a deeper understanding of how law enforcement and campus security responded to the crisis and what lessons were learned from this devastating event.

Reactions from Authorities During the Incident

The reactions from authorities during the April 17, 2025, shooting at Florida State University were swift, coordinated, and critical in preventing further casualties. Within minutes of the first gunshots, campus security, followed by local law enforcement, responded to the scene with urgency and professionalism. However, the chaos of the situation, the initial lack of information, and the sheer unpredictability of the event posed significant challenges that tested the effectiveness of their response.

Campus security was the first line of defense. As soon as the shots rang out, security personnel stationed around the Student Union were alerted. Their immediate priority was to ensure the safety of students and staff, evacuating as many people as possible from the building while simultaneously alerting law enforcement. They faced the daunting task of assessing the situation with little information and no clear sense of where the shooter was located. Campus security worked diligently to contain the area, evacuating nearby rooms and guiding students to secure locations. In the face of such an unpredictable and rapidly escalating situation, their actions were essential in minimizing the number of victims, though they could not prevent the initial violence.

Local law enforcement responded quickly, arriving on the scene within minutes of the first call to 911. Officers from both the FSU Police Department and the Tallahassee Police Department quickly coordinated their efforts to secure the building and neutralize the shooter. In the early moments of the attack, the officers were faced with a rapidly changing and dangerous environment. They had limited information only that gunfire had been heard at the Student Union and no clear sense of where the shooter was or how many victims had been injured. This uncertainty required law enforcement to act quickly and decisively.

Upon entering the building, officers immediately began clearing rooms and checking for casualties, working under the assumption that the shooter was still active and dangerous. They were methodical in their search, moving through the building while trying to minimize further harm. The police also worked to secure exits and provide immediate medical assistance to the injured, preventing additional deaths by ensuring that help arrived quickly. The critical decision to neutralize the shooter was made with urgency but was carried out with caution, as law enforcement officers knew that the situation could escalate at any moment.

In the moments after the shooter was apprehended, law enforcement turned their attention to securing the scene and assisting victims. Paramedics were quickly brought in to treat the injured, and officers worked with campus security to set up a perimeter, ensuring that no one else could enter the area. The response from authorities in those crucial minutes made all the difference in preventing additional violence and saving lives. However, it also revealed the challenges faced by law enforcement when responding to an active shooter situation with limited information and the rapid pace at which events were unfolding.

In retrospect, the reactions from authorities, though effective, also highlight the importance of preparedness and coordination. The lack of clarity in the early moments of the attack underscores the need for faster communication systems and more comprehensive training for campus security and law enforcement in active shooter scenarios. While the quick and decisive actions of the authorities were critical in preventing further loss of life, the situation emphasized the ongoing need for constant evaluation and improvement in response protocols.

How Law Enforcement Prevented Further Losses

Law enforcement's swift and decisive response during the Florida State University (FSU) shooting on April 17, 2025, played a crucial role in preventing further loss of life. As the first responders to arrive on the scene, local law enforcement officers faced an extremely high-pressure situation with limited information, making every decision critical. Despite these challenges, their coordinated actions ensured that the shooting was quickly brought to an end, minimizing the overall damage and saving countless lives.

Upon receiving the first 911 calls reporting the gunfire, law enforcement officers from the Tallahassee Police Department and the FSU Police Department immediately mobilized and rushed to the Student Union, where the attack was unfolding. The initial moments of their response were chaotic, as they had little to go on other than the fact that shots had been fired in a busy campus building. The uncertainty of the shooter's location, the number of victims, and the threat of further violence meant that officers had to make split-second decisions based on incomplete information. Despite this, they acted quickly to secure the perimeter, ensuring that no one else could enter the scene and adding a layer of control to a rapidly escalating situation.

Upon entering the building, law enforcement officers immediately began searching for the shooter. Their primary focus was to locate and neutralize the threat as quickly as possible. They moved systematically through the building, engaging in a process known as "room clearing," where each room was checked for the shooter or any additional threats. The decision to enter the building with such urgency, despite the risk to their own safety, was a critical moment that prevented further casualties. Officers were fully aware that the longer the shooter remained active, the greater the potential for more victims.

One of the key actions that helped prevent further loss of life was the speed at which law enforcement neutralized the threat. Within minutes of their arrival, they located Phoenix Ikner, the shooter, who had taken shelter in a secluded area of the building. Officers confronted him and swiftly apprehended him without further violence. The decisive actions taken by law enforcement ensured that no additional rounds were fired, and the threat was eliminated before the shooter could inflict more harm. The rapid intervention and immediate control of the situation were instrumental in limiting the impact of the shooting.

Furthermore, law enforcement played a crucial role in providing immediate medical assistance to the victims. As soon as the shooter was neutralized, officers and paramedics worked together to administer first aid, stabilize the injured, and get them to medical facilities as quickly as possible. The quick response of law enforcement in getting medical personnel into the building and organizing the evacuation of victims helped save many lives, preventing what could have been even greater casualties.

The actions of law enforcement during the FSU shooting exemplify the importance of swift, coordinated responses in active shooter situations. While the initial chaos and confusion could have easily resulted in further bloodshed, the decisive actions taken by police officers ensured that the situation was contained before it could spiral further out of control. Their focus on neutralizing the threat, combined with their commitment to securing the safety of the victims, played a vital role in preventing a far worse outcome. However, the event also raised important questions about the preparedness of campus security and law enforcement, highlighting the need for ongoing training and refinement of response protocols to ensure future incidents are handled as effectively as possible.

Evaluating the Effectiveness of Campus Security Protocols

The shooting at Florida State University (FSU) on April 17, 2025, highlighted both the strengths and weaknesses of the campus security protocols in place at the time. While the swift response of campus security and local law enforcement played a crucial role in minimizing casualties, the event also revealed significant gaps in how the university handled crisis situations. Evaluating the effectiveness of campus security protocols provides valuable insights into areas of improvement and underscores the need for universities to be better prepared for potential threats.

One of the most immediate concerns that emerged from the event was the ability of campus security to respond effectively within the first few minutes of the attack. While the university's security team acted quickly by alerting law enforcement and attempting to secure the building, their capacity to manage an active shooter situation was limited by the lack of real-time information. Campus security, although trained in general emergency procedures, was not fully equipped to handle the complexities of an active shooter scenario with such urgency and unpredictability. The absence of immediate access to detailed information about the shooter's location, weaponry, and the number of victims complicated their ability to act decisively at the onset of the crisis.

In terms of evacuation and containment efforts, campus security did make initial attempts to guide students to safety, but their ability to effectively manage large crowds in a panic situation was limited. Although some students were successfully evacuated or directed to secure locations, others were left trapped or without clear direction.

The chaos within the building, coupled with the limited resources available to campus security, made it difficult to quickly establish order and control the flow of people in and out of the building. The lack of a clearly defined and practiced evacuation plan for such a scenario became evident in this moment of crisis.

Another critical element in evaluating the effectiveness of campus security protocols is the university's communication system. During the incident, there were reports of confusion surrounding the dissemination of information, both internally among university staff and externally to the student body. While law enforcement had access to real-time data, campus security struggled to relay vital information to those inside the building and to the broader campus community. Timely alerts, clear directions, and constant updates are crucial in managing an emergency, yet the communication breakdown left many students uncertain about where to go for safety and what the specific threat was.

Moreover, the response of campus security in terms of coordination with local law enforcement could be described as reactive rather than proactive. Although the police arrived quickly on the scene, the initial coordination between campus security and law enforcement was not seamless. The lack of a unified, well-rehearsed plan between the two groups created a delay in neutralizing the shooter. Clearer collaboration and pre-established protocols could have reduced response time and ensured a more synchronized and efficient approach.

The tragedy at FSU also raised questions about the physical infrastructure and safety measures of the Student Union. While there were some security personnel on site, there were limited visible barriers, such as metal detectors or security checkpoints, that might have acted as deterrents for the shooter. The lack of stronger security measures, combined with open access to the building, made it easier for the shooter to enter the premises undetected and carry out his plan.

while the response of campus security during the FSU shooting undoubtedly saved lives, the event revealed several critical gaps in the university's preparedness for an active shooter situation. The lack of real-time information, ineffective communication, limited evacuation capabilities, and insufficient security infrastructure all contributed to the challenges faced during the crisis. The aftermath of the tragedy has led to widespread discussions on the need for universities to revise and improve their security protocols, invest in more comprehensive training for staff, and implement stronger measures to prevent such incidents from occurring in the future. The FSU incident serves as a stark reminder of the importance of continual evaluation and improvement of campus safety systems to protect the lives of students and faculty.

Part III

Aftermath and Reckoning

Chapter 8
Lives Lost and Lives Changed

The shooting at Florida State University on April 17, 2025, left a deep and irreversible impact on the lives of the victims, survivors, and their families. The immediate devastation of the tragedy was marked by the loss of innocent lives, but the aftermath revealed a much broader and more profound ripple effect on the entire FSU community. This chapter pays tribute to the victims, reflecting on their lives and the stories they left behind, while also delving into the experiences of those who survived the attack and the long journey to recovery they faced.

Each victim of the shooting was more than just a name or statistic; they were individuals with dreams, aspirations, and loved ones who now must carry the weight of their absence. The stories of the victims reflect the vibrant, promising lives that were tragically cut short. Their contributions to their families, friendships, and the FSU community will never be forgotten, and their memory continues to shape the healing process for those left behind.

For the survivors, the journey was equally harrowing. Many witnessed the violence firsthand, and the trauma they experienced would stay with them long after the shooter was apprehended. Some were physically injured, while others bore the invisible wounds of emotional and psychological scars. Their accounts of the incident, and the strength they found to recover and rebuild their lives, serve as a testament to human resilience in the face of unfathomable pain.

Finally, the tragedy extended beyond those directly involved, deeply affecting the families and friends of the victims. The lasting impact of such a loss is something that cannot be measured in days or months, but in years of emotional healing, remembrance, and the pursuit of justice. This chapter explores how those closest to the victims have coped with their grief and how the community has rallied around them in the aftermath of the tragedy.

A Tribute to Victims and Their Stories

The victims of the Florida State University (FSU) shooting on April 17, 2025, were not just random individuals caught in an unthinkable act of violence they were students, faculty, and staff who each had their own unique stories, aspirations, and dreams. Their lives, though tragically cut short, continue to be remembered by those who loved them and by the larger FSU community. This tribute honors their memory, reflecting on the impact they made in their short time and the ways in which their stories continue to inspire and drive change.

Among the victims were students who were just beginning their journeys toward their futures. They had hopes of graduation, careers, and contributing meaningfully to society. One victim was an aspiring journalist, passionate about storytelling and social justice. Another was a pre-med student, dedicated to becoming a doctor and helping others. There was a young woman who dreamed of becoming an artist, and a man who had just begun his journey in law, determined to make a difference in the world. Each of them was working toward a future that was suddenly taken from them. Their aspirations, though interrupted, are still remembered by those who knew them and by the FSU community at large, which now carries their hopes forward.

Equally important to remember are the faculty and staff who lost their lives. Some had dedicated decades to shaping the minds of students, offering guidance, and fostering intellectual growth. One of the victims was a beloved professor known for their unwavering commitment to students' success, while another worked behind the scenes to ensure that the campus ran smoothly, making an impact in ways often unseen. Their dedication to FSU's mission and the lives of their students left a profound mark on the university, and their loss has been felt deeply by colleagues and students alike.

The stories of these victims are not defined by the tragedy of their deaths but by the lives they lived before that fateful day. They were individuals who loved, worked, and dreamed. They were part of the fabric that made up the diverse and thriving community at FSU. The grief that followed the shooting is immeasurable, but so too is the sense of gratitude for having had them in the world, even for a short time.

In honoring these victims, FSU continues to remember their contributions and ensures that their stories are shared. The community has established memorials, scholarships, and tributes to keep their memories alive, reminding everyone that their lives were far more than just victims of violence. They were part of something greater, and their legacy continues to influence the university and the broader community in meaningful ways. Through the pain of loss, their stories have inspired resilience, a drive for change, and a commitment to preventing future tragedies. In remembering them, FSU honors their lives and ensures their spirits live on in the hearts of all who knew them.

Survivors' Accounts and the Road to Recovery

The survivors of the Florida State University shooting on April 17, 2025, carry with them not only the memories of the horrifying events they witnessed but also the painful journey of recovery that followed. For many, the physical injuries were just the beginning of a long and complicated process of healing one that involved grappling with emotional trauma, navigating the effects of post-traumatic stress, and finding a way to move forward after the attack that shattered their sense of security.

For some survivors, the immediate aftermath of the shooting was filled with confusion and disbelief. In the face of chaos, many did not initially realize the full extent of the tragedy. Their primary focus was survival seeking shelter, finding safety, and helping others along the way. Some survivors physically escaped the line of fire, while others were forced to witness the horror unfold around them. As the dust settled and the danger subsided, survivors began to process the reality of what had happened, leading to the emotional toll that would accompany them for months, even years, afterward.

The road to recovery was difficult and deeply personal for each survivor. Many experienced symptoms of post-traumatic stress disorder (PTSD), which manifested in a variety of ways. Flashbacks, anxiety, nightmares, and a constant sense of fear and vulnerability became part of daily life. Some survivors found it challenging to return to the very campus where the tragedy occurred, as even the familiar sights and sounds of FSU could trigger overwhelming emotions. The sense of loss and the absence of their peers weighed heavily on those who had survived, making the journey toward healing feel isolating at times.

Despite the emotional struggles, many survivors found strength in each other and in the support they received from their families, friends, and mental health professionals. Support groups for survivors of mass violence were established, providing them with a safe space to share their experiences and begin the process of healing together. For some, speaking out and sharing their stories publicly became an essential part of their recovery. It was through these acts of solidarity, where survivors supported one another, that many found the courage to take the first steps toward reclaiming their lives.

Physical recovery was another significant hurdle for many survivors. Some sustained severe injuries that required multiple surgeries and extensive rehabilitation. The path to regaining physical independence was long, but it was often aided by the unwavering support of family, friends, and medical professionals who helped them stay focused and motivated. For these survivors, healing became a journey of both body and mind.

Over time, many survivors found purpose in using their experiences to advocate for change, both at FSU and beyond. Some turned to activism, using their voices to push for reforms in campus safety and mental health services, while others chose to engage in public speaking or writing to share their stories and raise awareness about the long-term effects of mass violence. These survivors demonstrated incredible resilience, showing that while the physical and emotional scars of the shooting would never fully disappear, their ability to make a difference in the world was a powerful testament to their strength.

Ultimately, the survivors of the FSU shooting faced an arduous road to recovery, but through courage, support, and an unyielding desire to rebuild their lives, they found a way to move forward. Their accounts not only highlight the trauma that survivors endure but also the transformative power of community, advocacy, and healing. Their resilience continues to serve as an inspiration to those who face their own battles in the aftermath of tragedy.

The Lasting Impact on Families and Friends of the Victims

The lasting impact on the families and friends of the victims of the Florida State University shooting on April 17, 2025, is immeasurable. The trauma experienced by those closest to the victims extends far beyond the day of the shooting, with the emotional scars continuing to shape their lives in profound ways. For the families of the deceased, the sudden and violent loss of a loved one is something that no amount of time or therapy can ever fully erase. For friends, the loss of peers and companions in such a tragic and senseless way left a void that could never be filled. The ripple effects of this tragedy have changed the lives of those who loved and cared for the victims, leading them down a long and painful road of grief, healing, and resilience.

For the families, the shock of losing a child, sibling, or partner in such a traumatic event is something that many struggle to comprehend. Many of the victims were young adults, just beginning their journey in life, full of dreams and potential. Parents, siblings, and extended family members were left not only with the emotional burden of loss but with the overwhelming feeling of helplessness. The pain of having their loved ones taken so abruptly, under such horrific circumstances, has left many in a state of shock and disbelief. The road to healing for these families is complex and ongoing, as they attempt to make sense of the loss and navigate the aftermath. Grief can be isolating, and for many, the process is exacerbated by the public nature of the tragedy. These families were thrust into the national spotlight as the shooting unfolded, which added another layer of emotional strain as they were forced to grieve under public scrutiny.

Friends of the victims, too, experienced profound emotional trauma. The loss of close companions, many of whom were taken in the prime of their young adult lives, left their social circles shattered. The emotional toll of witnessing or hearing about the event was devastating for many friends who struggled with survivor's guilt, feelings of anger, and a deep sense of helplessness. For those who were injured, the emotional recovery often paralleled the physical one. But for those who escaped unharmed, the emotional weight was equally heavy. Many survivors wrestled with feelings of guilt for having survived when their friends did not. The trauma of losing someone in such a violent manner can change friendships, affecting how individuals view the world, trust others, and navigate relationships going forward.

The long-term impact on these families and friends has also been marked by a deep desire for justice and meaningful change. Many families and friends of the victims have channeled their grief into activism, advocating for stronger gun laws, improved campus safety measures, and greater mental health support for students. This desire for change became a way for them to honor the memories of their loved ones while working to prevent future tragedies from occurring. Their voices have become part of a broader conversation about gun violence and the need for systemic reforms to protect others from experiencing the same heartbreak.

Despite the pain, the families and friends of the victims have shown remarkable resilience. Their journey through grief, remembrance, and healing continues to be one of strength and courage. Their lives have been irrevocably changed, but through their collective efforts, they carry forward the memory of their loved ones, striving to ensure that their loss brings about positive change and greater awareness of the lasting impact of violence on families and communities.

Chapter 9
The Mourning Campus: Vigils and Solidarity

The aftermath of the Florida State University shooting on April 17, 2025, left the campus community devastated, yet the response to the tragedy also revealed the strength, resilience, and solidarity of those who were affected. In the face of such unimaginable grief, students, faculty, and staff came together in mourning, finding strength in one another as they navigated the difficult path toward healing. Vigils, memorials, and various acts of solidarity became the cornerstone of the collective grieving process, offering a way for the community to honor the victims and begin to rebuild.

This chapter examines how the FSU community responded to the tragedy through memorials, gatherings, and support for those directly affected by the shooting. Vigils held on campus became not only moments of reflection but also acts of unity, as individuals from all corners of the university students, faculty, staff, and alumni came together to remember the lives lost and show support for the survivors. These gatherings allowed the community to mourn collectively, offering a space for people to express their sorrow and share their commitment to moving forward in a way that honored the victims' memory.

Healing through collective grief became an essential part of the recovery process. For many, coming together as a community provided a sense of comfort, as it helped them feel less alone in their pain. It was through shared remembrance that many began to find a path to healing, offering and receiving support from one another in ways that would lay the foundation for future advocacy and resilience.

In addition to traditional memorials, social media played a significant role in organizing and amplifying the support that flooded in from both within the campus community and beyond. Social media platforms became a tool for organizing vigils, spreading messages of solidarity, and ensuring that the victims' stories were heard on a national stage. The role of social media in facilitating these memorial events and connecting people in their collective grief highlights how technology can be harnessed to provide support and solidarity in times of crisis.

Community Responses, Memorials, and National Support

In the wake of the Florida State University (FSU) shooting on April 17, 2025, the response from the campus community, local residents, and national supporters was a powerful demonstration of solidarity, compassion, and unity. The tragedy left a deep scar on the university, but the overwhelming wave of support that followed became a vital part of the healing process for the survivors, victims' families, and the broader FSU community. From heartfelt memorials to public demonstrations of grief, the collective response to the event provided an avenue for those affected to mourn, honor the victims, and come together in the face of unimaginable loss.

On campus, one of the first reactions was the organizing of vigils and memorial services. Students, faculty, and staff gathered in large numbers, lighting candles and holding hands to remember those lost in the shooting. The Student Union, which had been the site of the attack, became the focal point for much of this mourning. Makeshift memorials of flowers, photographs, and handwritten messages covered the building's walls, offering students a space to reflect and express their grief. The campus community collectively shared the emotional burden of the tragedy, finding comfort in each other's presence. These vigils were not only for remembering the victims but also for standing in solidarity with the survivors, who struggled with the trauma of the event.

Beyond the campus, support flooded in from across the nation. Universities, local communities, and individuals from all walks of life expressed their condolences through messages, fundraisers, and charitable acts. Donations poured in to support the families of the victims and the medical expenses of the injured, demonstrating the country's empathy for the FSU community. The outpouring of support from alumni, other universities, and national organizations was a testament to the wider impact of the tragedy, showing that the loss at FSU was not felt solely within the university but resonated across the country.

National and local organizations also showed their support by organizing events, such as candlelight vigils and rallies, to raise awareness about gun violence and advocate for changes to campus safety and mental health policies. These gatherings created a platform for students, faculty, and activists to express their grief and their desire for tangible change, further reinforcing the community's resolve to turn tragedy into a call for action. National media coverage ensured that the stories of the victims were heard far and wide, bringing attention to the issue of campus safety and encouraging broader conversations about gun control and mental health reform.

The community's responses both local and national provided a foundation for healing and rebuilding after the shooting. Memorials, public gatherings, and national support highlighted the resilience of the FSU community and the importance of coming together in the aftermath of such violence. The collective mourning not only honored the victims but also affirmed the commitment to a future where tragedies like this one are less likely to happen, fostering an environment where healing can take place and change can begin.

Healing through Collective Grief and Remembrance

Healing through collective grief and remembrance became a central theme for the Florida State University (FSU) community in the aftermath of the tragic shooting on April 17, 2025. In the wake of such an unimaginable event, the need for solidarity and shared mourning was crucial for the emotional recovery of those affected. While individual healing is necessary, the collective response allowed the campus and broader community to come together, offering each other support and understanding as they navigated their grief.

The process of collective grief began immediately after the shooting with organized vigils and memorial services. These gatherings provided students, faculty, staff, and survivors a space to come together, mourn, and honor the victims. The simple act of lighting candles or standing in silence was a powerful form of shared remembrance, as it allowed everyone to pay their respects and to reflect collectively on the profound loss. It was during these vigils that many found comfort in knowing that they were not alone in their sorrow. The strength of the community, united in its pain, helped many individuals feel supported during a time when isolation could have easily taken over.

One of the most profound aspects of collective grieving was the sense of connection it fostered. Survivors of the shooting, who faced the trauma of that day in different ways, were able to share their experiences and emotions with others who understood their pain. They found a space to express feelings of fear, confusion, and anger while being embraced by others who were equally affected by the tragedy. This communal environment facilitated emotional processing, allowing survivors to move through their trauma together, rather than alone. It provided the survivors with the opportunity to support one another in their shared journey toward recovery, reinforcing the sense of resilience that emerged in the wake of the tragedy.

For the families of the victims, collective remembrance was also an essential part of their healing process. The campus-wide tributes, memorial services, and public outpourings of love gave them a platform to mourn openly, while also providing them with the support of a broader community. Families found solace in the fact that their loved ones' lives were not defined solely by the violence of the shooting but were instead celebrated and remembered through the collective grief of the FSU community.

Furthermore, the act of remembering the victims in a shared, public way created a sense of continuity. The university community did not forget the victims, even as time passed. Memorials, both physical and symbolic, were established across campus to ensure that the memories of those lost would not fade. These memorials became spaces where students and faculty could visit, reflect, and remember, providing an ongoing reminder of the community's commitment to healing and remembrance.

As the weeks and months went by, the collective grieving process transitioned into a commitment to advocacy and action. Many members of the FSU community, inspired by their shared experience of loss, became vocal advocates for changes in gun laws and campus safety. By turning their grief into action, the community channeled their collective pain into a force for change, ensuring that the victims' lives and memories would continue to inspire efforts toward a safer and more compassionate future.

Healing through collective grief and remembrance at FSU demonstrated the power of community in the face of tragedy. It allowed individuals to mourn together, to process their pain, and to find strength in one another. The shared commitment to remembering the victims and advocating for change created a lasting legacy of unity, resilience, and hope that would carry the FSU community through the darkest days and into the future.

The Role of Social Media in Organizing Memorial Events

In the aftermath of the Florida State University (FSU) shooting on April 17, 2025, social media played a pivotal role in organizing memorial events and facilitating the grieving process for the campus community. Given the widespread use of social media platforms like Twitter, Facebook, and Instagram, these tools became essential in providing a platform for students, faculty, and the broader FSU community to organize, communicate, and support each other during a time of unprecedented tragedy.

Social media was instrumental in the immediate mobilization of memorial events. Within hours of the shooting, platforms such as Twitter and Facebook saw an outpouring of messages of support, as well as calls for action. Students, faculty, and alumni used hashtags to create a unified space for collective mourning and remembrance. These hashtags, such as #FSUstrong, became symbols of solidarity and resilience for the community, making it easier for people to find updates, share memories, and join in memorial events regardless of their location.

One of the most significant ways social media was used was in organizing and spreading information about vigils, memorial services, and campus-wide gatherings. In the absence of traditional communication methods, social media became the go-to platform for disseminating information quickly and efficiently. Student organizations, faculty, and even local community groups used social media to coordinate and publicize memorial services. Detailed information about the time, location, and purpose of vigils was shared widely, ensuring that students and faculty members could easily participate in the collective grief and healing process. The accessibility of this information made it possible for a larger group to participate in these events, including those who may have been physically unable to attend but still wanted to show support through virtual presence.

Social media also allowed survivors, family members, and those affected by the tragedy to share their stories, express their grief, and connect with others who were going through similar experiences. Platforms such as Instagram and Twitter gave people a voice, enabling them to honor the victims and memorialize their loved ones publicly. Survivors shared their personal experiences, while others posted pictures, messages, and tributes that celebrated the lives of those lost. This public expression of grief fostered a sense of shared experience, allowing people to feel connected and supported by a wider community that extended beyond FSU's campus.

Moreover, social media facilitated fundraising efforts for the victims' families and those who were injured. Crowdfunding platforms like GoFundMe were used to create fundraising campaigns, and these were heavily promoted through social media. The support for these campaigns came from not only FSU students and faculty but also from the larger national and international community, highlighting the power of social media to rally people together in times of crisis.

The role of social media in organizing memorial events also went beyond the immediate aftermath of the shooting. Over time, social media continued to serve as a space for ongoing healing, with individuals and groups using it to share progress, advocate for policy change, and create awareness about the broader issues of gun violence and campus safety. The ability to keep the conversation alive through these platforms ensured that the community's commitment to remember the victims and push for positive change would not fade away.

Chapter 10
Law Enforcement Under Scrutiny

In the wake of the Florida State University (FSU) shooting on April 17, 2025, law enforcement's response to the tragedy came under intense scrutiny. While the swift actions of campus security and local police undoubtedly prevented further casualties, the events also raised important questions about the effectiveness of their procedures, the adequacy of their training, and their ability to handle such a rapidly escalating crisis. This chapter explores the personal and professional responsibilities of law enforcement officers in the aftermath of the tragedy, examining how their actions were scrutinized and the subsequent investigations that sought to understand what went right and what could have been improved.

Immediately following the shooting, law enforcement officials were not only focused on securing the area, neutralizing the threat, and assisting victims but were also faced with the challenge of responding to public and media inquiries regarding their handling of the situation. While the actions of the officers who responded to the scene were widely praised for their speed and efficiency, questions remained about the preparedness of campus security and the communication between local law enforcement and university personnel. Investigations were launched to determine whether the response could have been more coordinated or quicker, and whether additional measures could have prevented the escalation.

In addition to the investigation, this chapter also discusses the reforms and changes in training that emerged as a result of the tragedy. The FSU shooting highlighted the need for law enforcement to continuously adapt their training to address the complexities of active shooter situations on college campuses. It became clear that the response protocols, while effective, required refinement to improve inter-agency communication, resource allocation, and overall readiness for such crises. The lessons learned from this incident would shape future law enforcement training programs and policies aimed at better equipping officers to handle similar emergencies. This chapter aims to assess these developments and their long-term impact on campus safety.

Personal and Professional Responsibilities in the Aftermath

In the aftermath of the Florida State University (FSU) shooting on April 17, 2025, the personal and professional responsibilities of law enforcement officers were scrutinized not only by the public but also within the law enforcement community itself. The tragic event, while swiftly contained due to the rapid response from local police and campus security, posed significant questions about the emotional and moral challenges that officers face during such high-pressure situations. Understanding the dual responsibilities of officers—both personal and professional—becomes key in evaluating their role in the aftermath of the tragedy.

On a personal level, law enforcement officers involved in responding to the shooting were forced to confront the emotional weight of the situation. Many officers were confronted with traumatic scenes, witnessing the direct effects of gun violence, interacting with victims, and attempting to assist those suffering from severe injuries. For some, the trauma of responding to such violence was compounded by the pressure of needing to remain composed and focused on their duties. The emotional toll of being involved in an incident that results in loss of life, even when the officers act with professionalism and speed, is often immense. Many officers reported feelings of distress, empathy for the victims, and even survivor's guilt, knowing that others might not have survived had their response been delayed. The responsibility of maintaining emotional control while processing such a traumatic event is a significant personal challenge, one that law enforcement agencies must address to ensure their officers are supported during the recovery process.

Professionally, law enforcement officers had a duty to respond efficiently and effectively under the chaotic and unpredictable conditions of the active shooter situation. The police were tasked with securing the area, neutralizing the threat, providing immediate care to the injured, and preventing further harm. In these moments, their training was put to the test. While their quick actions in locating and apprehending the shooter were praised, there were still questions raised about the overall coordination between campus security and local law enforcement, and whether the protocols in place were sufficient for the situation. Investigations into the response focused on areas where communication and coordination could have been improved. Some felt that better inter-agency collaboration, quicker information sharing, or even additional resources could have further minimized the threat or assisted in more efficient evacuations.

Moreover, law enforcement's professional responsibility extended beyond the immediate response to the crisis. They had to deal with the aftermath, engaging in critical investigations into the shooting, providing statements to the media, and answering to the public regarding their actions. Officers were expected to maintain transparency while also dealing with public pressure to assess whether their response could have been more effective. In addition to their official duties, law enforcement personnel had to continue fulfilling their ongoing professional roles—keeping the community safe while also ensuring that the lessons from the incident were internalized for future preparedness.

In the aftermath, law enforcement agencies began looking at reforms in response to the shooting. Many officers and administrators reflected on their own emotional processing of the event, realizing that mental health support for officers involved in traumatic events must be prioritized. Professionally, the tragedy served as a catalyst for revising and enhancing training protocols to ensure that law enforcement personnel were better equipped to handle not only the tactical aspects of active shooter situations but also the emotional complexities that accompany such events. The responsibility of law enforcement officers, both personal and professional, was to continue serving their communities while also ensuring they received the necessary support to cope with the profound emotional impact of such tragedies. The aftermath of FSU's shooting made it clear that law enforcement must balance both their personal emotional well-being and their professional duties to effectively serve their communities and prevent further loss.

Investigations into Law Enforcement's Handling of the Crisis

In the wake of the Florida State University (FSU) shooting on April 17, 2025, investigations into law enforcement's handling of the crisis became an essential part of understanding both the immediate response and the larger implications for campus safety and active shooter protocols. While the quick actions of law enforcement, particularly in neutralizing the shooter and providing aid to the wounded, were widely praised, several areas of concern emerged regarding the effectiveness of the response. These concerns prompted both internal and external investigations into the response protocols and the actions of campus security and local law enforcement.

One of the first areas of investigation focused on the response time and coordination between FSU's campus security and local law enforcement. While both groups responded rapidly, there were questions about the communication between campus security and police officers during the early stages of the crisis. Campus security, who were the first responders, initially had limited information and could not immediately pinpoint the shooter's location. As the situation unfolded, law enforcement officers arrived on the scene and took over the response. The issue of coordination between campus security and local police raised questions about whether there could have been better real-time communication and information sharing to allow for a more seamless response. Investigators examined whether there were gaps in inter-agency cooperation and if additional training or clearer protocols would have improved the handling of the situation.

Another key focus of the investigation was the effectiveness of the response strategies used by law enforcement. The immediate neutralization of the shooter was critical in preventing further loss of life, but the response also raised questions about the tactics employed by officers during the search for the shooter. Officers entered the building with limited information, and the initial confusion surrounding the situation meant that they had to operate with a high level of uncertainty. Investigators looked into whether the tactical decisions made during the active shooter response, such as entering the building without knowing the exact location of the shooter, were in line with best practices. The fast-moving nature of the crisis made it difficult to assess the situation in real time, yet it was essential to examine whether any tactical mistakes were made that could have endangered both officers and students.

Additionally, the handling of the aftermath of the crisis was scrutinized. Law enforcement's role in securing the campus, assisting victims, and providing information to the public was critical in the immediate hours following the attack. Investigations reviewed how effectively law enforcement communicated with students, faculty, and the public during this period. Were victims' families notified in a timely and respectful manner? Did law enforcement handle the release of information to the media appropriately? Ensuring transparency while balancing the need for sensitive information sharing became a complex issue for law enforcement agencies in the aftermath of the tragedy.

The investigations also highlighted the importance of preparing law enforcement for such crises. While the response on April 17, 2025, was commendable in many ways, the scrutiny of the situation led to calls for reforms in training and preparation. There was a consensus that training for active shooter situations should be more comprehensive, including better coordination between campus security and local law enforcement, clearer communication protocols, and more robust simulations of crisis scenarios. The findings of these investigations would go on to influence policies and practices not only at FSU but across other universities as well, as the nation sought ways to improve campus safety and law enforcement's ability to respond to active shooter situations.

The investigations into law enforcement's handling of the FSU shooting were critical for assessing the effectiveness of the response and identifying areas for improvement. While the actions of law enforcement prevented further casualties and ensured that the shooter was neutralized, the investigations underscored the complexities of managing a high-stakes crisis and highlighted the need for continued refinement of active shooter response protocols.

Reforms and Training After the Tragedy

In the aftermath of the Florida State University (FSU) shooting on April 17, 2025, both law enforcement and campus security recognized the need for comprehensive reforms and improved training to better prepare for future crises. While the quick response from law enforcement was essential in preventing further loss of life, the tragedy highlighted significant gaps in protocols, communication, and preparedness that needed to be addressed to ensure the safety of students, faculty, and staff in the event of future emergencies.

One of the immediate areas identified for reform was the coordination between campus security and local law enforcement. While both entities responded quickly, the investigation into the incident revealed that communication between them could have been more streamlined. Campus security, often the first to respond in a campus crisis, had limited information and was not always equipped with the resources or authority to manage the situation until law enforcement arrived. This lack of coordination slowed the response in the critical first few minutes. In response to this, new training initiatives were implemented that focused on fostering stronger communication between campus security and local law enforcement. Joint exercises and simulations were created to practice coordinated responses, ensuring that officers from both groups would work seamlessly together during an active shooter scenario.

In addition to improving coordination, law enforcement agencies began to reevaluate their active shooter response protocols. The tragedy underscored the need for law enforcement officers to be better trained in handling fast-moving and chaotic situations with limited information. Training now includes more realistic simulations of active shooter events, incorporating the unpredictability of real-world scenarios. Officers are trained to make rapid decisions under pressure while ensuring that they can communicate effectively with their teams, campus officials, and other first responders. Special emphasis is placed on tactics that prioritize minimizing harm to bystanders, ensuring the safety of victims, and neutralizing the threat as quickly as possible.

Another critical reform was the focus on mental health awareness and emotional support for law enforcement officers involved in such high-stress events. The traumatic nature of responding to a mass shooting can leave lasting emotional scars on officers, and their mental health was recognized as a critical component of post-incident recovery. As a result, new protocols were put in place to provide mental health support and counseling for officers following critical incidents. This included mandatory debriefings after major events, where officers could discuss the emotional impact of the situation and receive professional psychological support. Recognizing the toll these events take on officers' well-being is essential for ensuring that they can continue to serve effectively without enduring long-term emotional harm.

On the university side, FSU implemented new training programs for faculty and staff to better prepare them for emergency situations. This included active shooter drills, training in how to recognize and respond to warning signs of violence, and how to assist students in coping with trauma. Faculty members were given tools to help students during and after a crisis, learning how to provide basic first aid, manage stress in a high-pressure environment, and offer emotional support to those affected by the incident. These programs were also designed to foster a culture of awareness and proactive engagement, encouraging staff and students to report any concerns that might indicate a potential threat.

Finally, the reforms included a review of campus security measures, particularly regarding physical security on campus. While the university had security personnel in place, the shooting revealed the need for enhanced security infrastructure, such as better surveillance systems, more visible security presence during peak hours, and the installation of lockdown systems in academic buildings. These changes were aimed at creating a more secure environment for students and staff, while also fostering a sense of safety in the aftermath of the tragedy.

The reforms and training implemented after the FSU shooting reflect a comprehensive effort to address the shortcomings revealed by the tragedy. The focus on improving coordination between campus security and law enforcement, enhancing active shooter training, providing mental health support for officers, and strengthening university preparedness are all critical steps toward creating a safer and more resilient campus environment. These changes, while born out of a painful tragedy, reflect a commitment to preventing future loss and ensuring that communities can better respond to such crises in the future.

Chapter 11
Mental Health and Responsibility

The tragic shooting at Florida State University (FSU) on April 17, 2025, underscored the critical intersection between mental health and violence prevention. In the aftermath of the event, questions arose about the role mental health played in both the development of the shooter's distress and the broader responsibility of institutions in preventing such tragedies. This chapter explores how mental health factors into the responsibility for preventing violence on campus, particularly the need for early intervention and robust support systems.

One of the key issues highlighted by the FSU tragedy is the failure to recognize the signs of mental health distress early enough to intervene. Phoenix Ikner's escalating emotional turmoil, which was evident in his behavior, social media posts, and isolation, went largely unnoticed by those around him. This chapter examines how earlier intervention could have potentially altered the trajectory of his life and prevented the violence he ultimately perpetrated. It also looks at the importance of providing accessible mental health resources and support systems that can help students navigate personal challenges before they reach a crisis point.

Additionally, the stigma surrounding mental health on college campuses often prevents students from seeking help, despite the pressures they face. The fear of being judged or misunderstood can stop students from accessing the resources they need, which is why promoting mental health awareness and reducing stigma is crucial in creating an environment where students feel empowered to reach out for help. This chapter delves into the importance of fostering a culture of openness around mental health, both within the campus community and through institutional policies.

By examining the role of mental health in violence prevention, the chapter calls for a systemic shift toward greater emphasis on early intervention, accessible support, and a more supportive campus environment. The ultimate goal is to ensure that no student feels isolated or unsupported to the point of taking destructive actions, and that mental health is treated with the same urgency and care as any other aspect of student well-being.

The Role of Mental Health in Prevention and Accountability

The role of mental health in the prevention and accountability of violent acts, particularly in the context of campus shootings like the one at Florida State University (FSU) on April 17, 2025, cannot be overstated. Mental health is a crucial factor in understanding why individuals may engage in violent behavior and, equally important, how to prevent such acts before they occur. In the case of Phoenix Ikner, the shooter, his mental health struggles were clear signs of a deeper issue that, if addressed earlier, might have helped avoid the tragedy. Examining the intersection between mental health, prevention, and accountability can provide critical insights into how similar events can be prevented in the future.

Mental health is often a complex and contributing factor in violent behavior. In the case of Phoenix, there were clear indicators that he was struggling with emotional distress, isolation, and anger, yet these signs were largely ignored or misunderstood by those around him. His psychological state marked by withdrawal, mood swings, and social media posts hinting at violence was a red flag that, if recognized, could have prompted intervention. Mental health issues such as untreated depression, anxiety, and unresolved trauma can lead to emotional instability, and in some cases, to violent outbursts. Understanding that mental health struggles are not just personal issues, but often part of larger societal and institutional challenges, is essential in addressing their role in violence.

One of the key lessons from the FSU tragedy is the need for early intervention. Had Phoenix received support earlier whether through counseling, mental health resources, or simply more engaged relationships with those around him his emotional distress might have been addressed before it escalated. Early intervention can provide individuals with the tools they need to manage their emotions and cope with personal challenges. Campus environments, however, often fail to provide sufficient access to mental health resources, either because students are unaware of the services available or are afraid to seek help due to stigma.

The responsibility for addressing mental health challenges lies not only with the individual but also with institutions, such as universities, that are tasked with supporting students' well-being. Universities should be proactive in providing accessible mental health services, creating a culture that encourages students to seek help, and ensuring that warning signs of mental distress are identified early. Faculty and staff play a critical role in noticing changes in students' behavior and providing support or directing them to proper resources. Institutions must prioritize mental health as part of their overall commitment to student safety and academic success.

Furthermore, accountability is a crucial element in the discussion of mental health and violence prevention. Mental health care systems, campus policies, and law enforcement all have roles in ensuring that students like Phoenix do not slip through the cracks. Accountability is not only about holding individuals responsible but also about ensuring institutions are equipped and responsive to students' mental health needs. If campus security, faculty, and law enforcement had recognized the severity of Phoenix's emotional distress, his access to firearms might have been prevented, and the tragedy could have been avoided.

Addressing mental health in the context of violence prevention is a multifaceted responsibility. It requires early recognition of signs of distress, accessible and effective mental health support systems, and a cultural shift that reduces stigma and encourages seeking help. Universities, law enforcement, and society as a whole must work together to prevent such tragedies by placing greater emphasis on mental health care and taking responsibility for the well-being of individuals within their communities. Understanding the role of mental health in prevention and accountability is vital for creating safer campuses and fostering environments where students feel supported and heard.

The Importance of Early Intervention and Support Systems

The importance of early intervention and support systems in preventing tragedies like the Florida State University (FSU) shooting on April 17, 2025, cannot be overstated. Early intervention plays a crucial role in identifying individuals who may be struggling with emotional or psychological issues, helping to prevent those issues from escalating into violent actions. For individuals like Phoenix Ikner, who exhibited signs of distress long before the shooting, early identification and appropriate support could have been the key to altering the trajectory of his life and preventing the violence that occurred.

One of the critical elements of early intervention is recognizing the warning signs of mental distress. Phoenix's behavior leading up to the shooting his social withdrawal, mood swings, and alarming social media posts was indicative of someone who was struggling internally. However, those around him, including friends, family, and university staff, did not recognize the severity of his struggles or did not intervene in a way that could have made a difference. Early intervention programs are designed to identify such signs early, enabling individuals to receive the help they need before their emotional distress spirals into more dangerous behaviors. This could involve offering counseling, mental health services, or simply creating a supportive environment where individuals feel comfortable reaching out for help.

The role of support systems in this process is equally important. A well-structured support system provides individuals with a network of people and resources they can turn to when they are in distress. At universities, this support system should include accessible mental health resources, peer counseling programs, and faculty who are trained to identify mental health issues. Students should be encouraged to utilize these services without fear of judgment or stigma. A proactive and engaged approach from faculty and staff, combined with a culture that promotes well-being, can create an environment where students feel safe asking for help and are more likely to do so before they reach a crisis point.

Support systems also play a vital role in continuing care after initial intervention. Simply identifying a mental health issue is not enough; individuals need consistent support to ensure that they can manage their challenges over time. This support can come in the form of ongoing therapy, academic accommodations, or group counseling sessions that provide a sense of belonging and community. For Phoenix, consistent support and mental health care may have prevented the build-up of anger and isolation that contributed to his violent actions.

Another critical aspect of early intervention is addressing the stigma that often surrounds mental health. Many students, including Phoenix, may have been hesitant to seek help due to fear of being labeled or judged. By fostering a campus culture that normalizes mental health struggles and encourages open dialogue, universities can break down the barriers that prevent students from reaching out for support. Peer-led programs, mental health awareness campaigns, and visible support resources can help reduce stigma and create a more inclusive and empathetic environment.

The importance of early intervention and strong support systems cannot be ignored in preventing violence on college campuses. When students are identified early and provided with the right resources and emotional support, they are better equipped to cope with challenges in healthy, non-violent ways. By prioritizing mental health, reducing stigma, and ensuring that support systems are accessible and effective, institutions can help prevent future tragedies and foster a safer, more supportive environment for all students. Early intervention is not just a preventive measure but a fundamental approach to protecting the mental well-being of individuals before crisis points are reached.

Addressing Stigma and Promoting Mental Health Awareness on Campus

Addressing stigma and promoting mental health awareness on college campuses is a crucial component of creating a supportive environment where students feel empowered to seek help and engage with mental health resources before their struggles escalate into crises. In the wake of tragedies like the Florida State University (FSU) shooting on April 17, 2025, it becomes clear that the stigma surrounding mental health and the reluctance to seek help can contribute to the intensity of a situation. Students, like Phoenix Ikner, may suffer in silence because they fear being judged or labeled, ultimately resulting in catastrophic consequences. Breaking down these barriers and fostering an environment of openness, support, and understanding is key to preventing similar tragedies.

Stigma surrounding mental health often arises from misconceptions and societal attitudes that associate mental illness with weakness or instability. On many college campuses, students may hesitate to seek help for fear of being perceived as "crazy" or "different." This stigma can create an atmosphere of silence around mental health issues, leaving students to suffer in isolation without the support they need. Addressing this stigma involves shifting the narrative surrounding mental health, framing it as an essential aspect of overall well-being rather than something to be hidden or ashamed of. Universities have an opportunity to lead this change by promoting open conversations about mental health, emphasizing that struggles with mental health are common and should be addressed with the same seriousness as physical health concerns.

Promoting mental health awareness on campus is an essential step in combating stigma. This involves creating widespread education campaigns that focus on recognizing the signs of mental distress, understanding the available resources, and encouraging students to take proactive steps to care for their mental health. Through workshops, seminars, and informational campaigns, students can be educated about the importance of seeking help early, and about the resources available to them, including counseling services, peer support groups, and mental health hotlines. By normalizing these conversations, students are more likely to reach out when they feel overwhelmed or distressed, as they will not fear judgment or feel like they are the only ones struggling.

The university can also integrate mental health education into their broader student wellness programs. Having mental health as part of orientation programs, resident advisor training, and student leadership development helps make mental health an ongoing conversation rather than something that's addressed only when problems arise. In these settings, students can learn how to identify early signs of mental health issues not just in themselves but also in others, helping to create a culture of support and empathy.

One of the most impactful ways to address mental health stigma is through peer support programs. Students often feel more comfortable speaking with their peers, who may have similar experiences or understand the challenges of campus life. By training students to be peer counselors or offering mental health first-aid courses, universities can create a system of support that is rooted in empathy and shared experience. Peer support programs can also reduce the feelings of isolation that many students face when they are struggling with their mental health.

Ultimately, addressing stigma and promoting mental health awareness requires a multi-faceted approach that involves the entire campus community students, faculty, staff, and administrators. It is not enough to provide resources; the culture surrounding mental health must change. When mental health is normalized, understood, and treated with the same importance as physical health, students are more likely to seek help and access the support they need before a crisis unfolds. In doing so, universities can help prevent future tragedies and create a safer, more supportive environment for all students.

Part IV

Toward Healing and Change

Chapter 12
Guns and Campuses: A National Debate Rekindled

The Florida State University (FSU) shooting on April 17, 2025, reignited a national debate on the intersection of gun laws, campus safety, and the role of legal responsibility in preventing mass shootings. The tragedy, like so many others, raised crucial questions about the accessibility of firearms, particularly in environments like university campuses, where students are supposed to feel safe. In the aftermath of the shooting, discussions surrounding gun laws became more urgent, as the event highlighted the gaps in existing regulations and the potential for stronger policies to prevent similar tragedies.

This chapter explores the renewed discussions on gun laws in the wake of the FSU tragedy, examining how the shooting spurred a deeper examination of both state and federal policies regarding firearm accessibility. The debate on whether stricter gun control measures could have prevented the shooting is complex, but it remains central to the conversation about preventing future incidents. Similarly, the discussion surrounding campus safety has become more urgent, with universities rethinking their security protocols, policies regarding concealed carry, and overall preparedness in the event of an active shooter situation.

Moreover, political advocacy groups have played a significant role in shaping the discourse around gun laws and campus safety. These organizations, which often represent diverse viewpoints, have pushed for stronger regulations and reform, sometimes clashing over what constitutes the most effective policy to protect students while respecting Second Amendment rights. This chapter delves into the role of political advocacy groups in influencing both public opinion and legislative change, exploring how their efforts have contributed to the ongoing debate and, in some cases, led to changes in policy or heightened awareness about the issues at hand.

Through these discussions, this chapter highlights the critical need for a balanced approach to gun laws, campus safety, and political activism, aiming to ensure that universities remain safe spaces for learning while addressing the broader concerns about gun violence in America.

Renewed Discussions on Gun Laws Post-Tragedy

The tragedy at Florida State University (FSU) on April 17, 2025, sparked renewed and intense discussions about gun laws across the United States. With another mass shooting on a college campus, the debate surrounding the accessibility of firearms and the need for stricter gun control reached a fever pitch. While the incident reignited calls for greater regulation of firearms, it also underscored the complexities of balancing public safety with constitutional rights, particularly in the context of higher education.

Following the FSU shooting, many advocates for stricter gun laws argued that the event highlighted the urgent need for comprehensive reforms to prevent similar tragedies in the future. One of the key points in this renewed discussion was the ease with which Phoenix Ikner, the shooter, was able to legally purchase a firearm despite the signs of emotional distress he had exhibited in the months leading up to the attack. His ability to obtain a weapon raised critical questions about the effectiveness of background checks, especially when it comes to screening for mental health issues. Advocates for stronger regulations pushed for more stringent background checks that would include mental health evaluations, closing loopholes in existing laws that allow individuals with clear signs of distress or violence to legally acquire firearms.

In particular, discussions focused on the need to raise the legal age for purchasing certain types of firearms, expand waiting periods, and introduce mandatory training for gun buyers. The lack of a comprehensive federal framework to regulate gun sales and ownership has been a longstanding issue, and tragedies like the FSU shooting have reinvigorated calls for a national standard. At the state level, some regions moved to introduce laws that would prohibit individuals with documented mental health struggles from obtaining firearms, although the effectiveness of these laws remains debated.

Opponents of stricter gun laws, including Second Amendment advocates, argued that such measures would infringe upon the constitutional rights of law-abiding citizens and would not necessarily prevent mass shootings. They point to the potential for self-defense and the idea that responsible gun ownership is a safeguard against crime. Some argue that the focus should instead be on improving mental health support and campus security, rather than on limiting access to firearms. This tension between upholding constitutional rights and ensuring public safety remains at the heart of the national gun debate.

In the wake of the FSU shooting, various national and state-level gun control organizations, such as Everytown for Gun Safety and the Brady Campaign, ramped up their advocacy efforts. They pushed for federal action, including the reinstatement of the assault weapons ban, restrictions on high-capacity magazines, and other gun safety measures. Their campaigns gained traction, with public opinion shifting toward supporting stronger gun laws, particularly in the wake of repeated mass shootings.

However, the challenge of implementing widespread reform is compounded by deeply entrenched political divisions. The influence of powerful gun rights organizations, such as the National Rifle Association (NRA), continues to shape the debate, often blocking or watering down proposed legislation. Despite growing public support for reform, political gridlock has slowed meaningful change, with lawmakers on both sides of the aisle struggling to find common ground.

The renewed discussions on gun laws post-FSU tragedy reflect the broader, ongoing debate about how to balance public safety with the protection of individual rights. The shooting underscored the need for comprehensive reform, including stronger background checks and restrictions on gun access, but the path to meaningful change remains fraught with political and ideological challenges. The debate will likely continue to shape the national conversation about gun violence for years to come.

Debates on Campus Safety and Legal Responsibility

The tragic shooting at Florida State University (FSU) on April 17, 2025, ignited widespread debates surrounding campus safety and the legal responsibilities of universities, law enforcement, and the individuals involved. This incident forced a critical examination of how campuses should prepare for active shooter situations, the policies regarding gun access on campus, and the legal obligations of both university officials and law enforcement to protect students and staff. The conversation on campus safety became multifaceted, encompassing issues of security protocols, prevention strategies, and accountability, all within the legal context of student rights and the broader national gun laws debate.

One of the key aspects of the debate was whether universities should implement stricter security measures, including increased surveillance, armed security personnel, or even allowing concealed carry on campuses. FSU, like many other universities, had security protocols in place, but the shooting highlighted that these measures were not sufficient to prevent or mitigate the effects of a shooting in a crowded, public space. Campus safety advocates argued that universities needed to adopt more comprehensive strategies that involved more than just emergency response plans. These would include integrating technology such as real-time surveillance systems, mass notification systems, and lockdown capabilities that could quickly alert students and faculty during a crisis. Additionally, increasing the visible presence of trained security officers would act as a deterrent to potential threats and provide immediate assistance when necessary.

On the other side of the debate, gun rights advocates argued that allowing students and staff to carry firearms on campus could enhance safety, giving individuals the means to defend themselves in an active shooter situation. The controversy surrounding this issue is rooted in the legal rights of gun owners, particularly under the Second Amendment, and the belief that individuals should be able to protect themselves from harm. However, opponents of concealed carry on campus argued that introducing more firearms could create additional risks, especially given the potential for confusion during an active shooter situation, where the presence of multiple armed individuals could complicate the actions of law enforcement.

Legally, universities face a responsibility to ensure the safety of students while also respecting their rights. This responsibility includes implementing policies that balance security measures with students' constitutional rights, such as the right to free speech, the right to privacy, and the right to protection from discrimination. After the FSU shooting, many questioned whether universities were doing enough to address mental health concerns and prevent violent acts before they occur. Critics pointed out that while law enforcement responded quickly, universities could have done more in terms of prevention. Had there been stronger mental health support systems, better identification of warning signs, and a more effective way of intervening with students at risk, the tragedy might have been prevented.

The legal implications also extended to the question of accountability. In the wake of the shooting, many wondered whether the university, law enforcement, or both were liable for failing to prevent the attack. Questions were raised about whether more could have been done to intervene earlier in Phoenix Ikner's troubled mental state or to limit his access to firearms. Some called for stricter campus gun control policies, arguing that universities should have more authority to regulate firearms on their campuses, while others argued that universities should focus on providing more mental health resources and enhancing student outreach programs.

The debates on campus safety and legal responsibility after the FSU shooting underscored the complexity of balancing the need for security with the legal and ethical considerations of individual rights. The tragedy led to renewed discussions about how universities should handle active shooter situations, whether stricter security measures should be implemented, and how legal frameworks surrounding gun ownership and campus safety need to evolve to better protect students and faculty. These debates, while difficult, are essential in shaping the future of campus safety and ensuring that higher education institutions are prepared to prevent and respond to crises effectively.

The Role of Political Advocacy Groups in Shaping Policy

The role of political advocacy groups in shaping policy following tragedies like the Florida State University (FSU) shooting is instrumental in driving legislative change and raising public awareness on critical issues such as gun violence, campus safety, and mental health. These organizations, often comprised of survivors, families, and concerned citizens, work tirelessly to push for reforms that address the root causes of such violence and prevent future tragedies. Their efforts are crucial in translating public outrage into policy action, as they advocate for changes at local, state, and federal levels.

Political advocacy groups like Everytown for Gun Safety, the Brady Campaign, and Moms Demand Action have long been at the forefront of pushing for stricter gun laws and advocating for broader reforms. In the wake of the FSU shooting, these organizations worked quickly to mobilize public opinion and channel it into concrete action. Their primary focus has been on promoting stricter gun control measures, including universal background checks, restrictions on assault weapons, and more stringent laws around gun ownership. These groups have emphasized the importance of closing loopholes in the current system, such as the gun show loophole, which allows firearms to be sold without background checks, thereby enabling individuals with criminal records or mental health issues to obtain guns more easily.

In addition to gun control, political advocacy groups have also focused on reforming policies related to campus safety and mental health. Recognizing the vulnerability of college campuses to mass shootings, these groups have called for stronger security measures, including increased funding for campus police, better emergency preparedness training, and improvements in surveillance systems. Moreover, these organizations have pushed for expanded mental health resources on campuses, arguing that early intervention and accessible counseling services can prevent violent behavior before it escalates.

Advocacy groups also play a key role in educating the public about the effects of gun violence and the need for reform. Through media campaigns, petitions, and public demonstrations, these groups work to maintain public attention on the issue, ensuring that the conversation about gun violence does not fade from the national discourse. They also work to mobilize constituents, urging them to contact lawmakers, participate in protests, and vote for candidates who support stronger gun control measures.

Perhaps one of the most significant roles these groups play is in lobbying lawmakers and influencing public policy. Their efforts often include organizing direct meetings with elected officials, providing testimonies in hearings, and working with legal experts to draft legislation. Political advocacy groups also collaborate with grassroots organizations, local activists, and survivors to create a broad coalition of voices demanding change. Through their tireless work, these groups help shift the political landscape, making it clear to lawmakers that gun violence prevention is a critical issue that demands legislative action.

In the context of the FSU shooting, these advocacy groups have pushed for reforms that would specifically address issues unique to campus shootings. For instance, they have advocated for regulations on concealed carry laws on college campuses, arguing that more guns in academic settings may exacerbate the problem rather than mitigate it. Similarly, they have called for stronger federal oversight of campus security policies to ensure that universities are better equipped to handle active shooter situations.

Chapter 13
Rebuilding Trust and Security at FSU

The aftermath of the Florida State University (FSU) shooting on April 17, 2025, left the campus community shaken, but it also sparked a critical reevaluation of campus security, student safety, and institutional responsibility. In the wake of such a devastating event, FSU was faced with the task of rebuilding trust and restoring a sense of safety and security on campus. This chapter explores the institutional changes and reforms that were implemented to improve student safety, enhance counseling and support services, and reassess FSU's emergency response protocols to ensure that the university was better equipped to prevent and respond to future crises.

The university's leadership recognized that the trauma of the shooting extended far beyond the immediate loss and injuries; it also fractured the sense of security that students, faculty, and staff once took for granted. As a result, FSU took decisive steps to address the gaps in campus security, revisiting everything from physical security measures to policies surrounding mental health and crisis intervention. These reforms aimed not only to prevent future tragedies but also to create a campus environment where students felt safe, supported, and empowered to seek help when needed.

Equally important in the recovery process were the enhancements to counseling and support services, which were critical for students, faculty, and staff who needed help processing their emotions, grief, and trauma. The university expanded its mental health resources, ensuring that students had access to counseling and peer support systems designed to address the psychological fallout from the shooting.

Finally, this chapter addresses how FSU revisited and revised its emergency response protocols. By learning from the shooting, the university worked to improve communication, coordination, and overall preparedness in the face of emergencies. The goal was to ensure that in the event of another crisis, FSU could respond more effectively, mitigating harm and providing swift support to those affected. Through these reforms, FSU aimed to rebuild the campus community and strengthen its commitment to student safety, ensuring that the lessons learned from the tragedy would lead to lasting change.

Institutional Changes and Student Safety Reforms

In the wake of the tragic shooting at Florida State University (FSU) on April 17, 2025, the university undertook significant institutional changes and safety reforms aimed at rebuilding trust and enhancing the security of the campus community. The impact of the event reverberated across every corner of the university, forcing leadership to reassess its safety protocols, campus infrastructure, and overall preparedness. The primary objective was to create an environment where students, faculty, and staff could feel safe while also ensuring that the university was better equipped to handle potential threats in the future.

One of the first steps FSU took was to evaluate and improve its physical security measures. The Student Union, where the shooting occurred, was the focal point for these changes. New security systems were put in place, including enhanced surveillance cameras, better lighting around campus, and the installation of panic buttons in high-risk areas. The university also increased the presence of trained security personnel, especially in areas with heavy student foot traffic. Security personnel were given additional training in active shooter protocols and emergency response strategies to ensure a swift and coordinated response in the event of another crisis.

In addition to strengthening physical security, FSU recognized the need to overhaul its emergency response systems. The university's emergency notification system was updated to allow for faster, more effective communication during a crisis. Students, faculty, and staff were provided with clear guidelines on how to respond to an active shooter situation, including evacuation routes and safe zones. Additionally, FSU worked closely with local law enforcement to ensure better coordination between campus security and police forces in any future emergency situations. Regular active shooter drills and simulations were incorporated into the university's safety protocol, helping to prepare everyone on campus for the unthinkable.

Another key aspect of the reforms was a renewed focus on mental health and support services. The trauma of the shooting left many students, faculty, and staff grappling with grief, anxiety, and post-traumatic stress. FSU expanded its counseling services, hiring additional mental health professionals and offering more peer support programs. The university also increased efforts to raise awareness about mental health resources available on campus and encouraged students to seek help if needed. Campus-wide mental health campaigns were launched to reduce the stigma surrounding seeking counseling and to promote well-being as a part of overall academic success.

Additionally, FSU revisited its policies around campus access and gun control. While Florida state law allows for the legal possession of firearms, the university imposed more stringent rules regarding weapons on campus, focusing on both preventive measures and emergency procedures. The university engaged in ongoing dialogue with local lawmakers, law enforcement, and student organizations to ensure that campus safety policies aligned with the needs of the community and state regulations.

Finally, FSU implemented a broader student safety initiative aimed at fostering a sense of community and collective responsibility. Students were encouraged to be more vigilant and proactive in reporting any suspicious behavior. Peer support networks were bolstered, and student organizations worked together to create a more inclusive, supportive campus environment. The goal was to create a culture where students not only felt physically safe but also emotionally supported in navigating their academic and personal lives.

FSU's institutional changes and student safety reforms were multifaceted and comprehensive. From physical security upgrades to improvements in emergency response protocols and mental health support services, the university sought to address the immediate and long-term needs of its community. These changes were aimed at preventing future tragedies, rebuilding trust, and ensuring that the campus remained a safe place for students to learn, grow, and thrive. The lessons learned from the tragedy were not taken lightly, and the reforms put in place were a testament to FSU's commitment to student safety and well-being.

The Role of Counseling and Support Services in Campus Recovery

In the aftermath of the Florida State University (FSU) shooting on April 17, 2025, the role of counseling and support services became a central element in the campus recovery process. The emotional and psychological toll of such a traumatic event was felt deeply by students, faculty, staff, and survivors, making access to mental health services crucial for healing. Recognizing the severity of the situation, FSU took immediate action to expand and strengthen its counseling services, ensuring that everyone on campus had the necessary resources to process their grief, trauma, and emotional struggles.

One of the first steps FSU took was to increase the availability of mental health professionals. The university hired additional counselors and therapists, specifically trained to handle trauma, grief, and crisis intervention. These professionals were available around the clock, providing immediate support for those affected by the shooting. Whether it was one-on-one therapy sessions, group counseling, or crisis intervention, the expanded counseling services offered students, faculty, and staff a safe space to talk about their experiences, express their emotions, and receive guidance on how to cope with the aftermath of the tragedy.

Peer support networks also played an integral role in the recovery process. Recognizing that students may be more likely to seek help from their peers, FSU increased efforts to train students as peer counselors and support leaders. These peer support programs allowed students to connect with others who had shared similar experiences or emotions, creating an environment where individuals could find solidarity and understanding. Peer counselors facilitated group therapy sessions, emotional check-ins, and informal support groups, which became critical to helping students feel less isolated in their grief and trauma.

In addition to individual counseling and peer support, FSU launched a series of campus-wide mental health awareness campaigns. These campaigns were designed to reduce the stigma surrounding mental health issues, encouraging students to seek help without fear of judgment. Posters, social media posts, and awareness events promoted the availability of mental health resources and normalized the conversation around mental well-being. The goal was to create a culture on campus where seeking help was seen as a sign of strength, not weakness. By addressing mental health openly and inclusively, FSU aimed to reduce barriers to care and make it easier for students to access the support they needed.

The emotional and psychological impact of the tragedy did not just affect those directly involved in the shooting, but also extended to the broader campus community. Faculty and staff, who had witnessed the events or had students and colleagues impacted by the tragedy, were also provided with counseling services. FSU recognized that educators and campus employees played a critical role in supporting students, and therefore, they needed their own avenues for processing their grief and emotional distress. By offering counseling to faculty and staff, the university ensured that they were not only able to care for themselves but could also better support their students through the recovery process.

Additionally, FSU expanded its outreach efforts to ensure that students who were at risk of experiencing ongoing trauma or mental health issues were continuously monitored and supported. Long-term follow-up care was offered to survivors and those who had experienced significant emotional distress. For some, recovery was a gradual process that required ongoing support, and FSU ensured that these resources were available well after the immediate crisis.

Counseling and support services played an essential role in the recovery process at FSU following the tragic shooting. By increasing the availability of mental health professionals, training peer counselors, and launching awareness campaigns, the university created a comprehensive support system that helped students, faculty, and staff navigate their grief, trauma, and emotional challenges. These services were vital in fostering a culture of care and resilience on campus, allowing the FSU community to heal collectively while ensuring that individuals received the personal support they needed to recover from the trauma of that day.

Revisiting FSU's Emergency Response Protocols

In the wake of the Florida State University (FSU) shooting on April 17, 2025, a critical review of the university's emergency response protocols became necessary. The tragedy underscored the importance of preparedness, coordination, and communication during a crisis, prompting FSU to revisit and revise its procedures to better respond to future emergencies. The goal was not only to evaluate what went wrong but also to identify areas for improvement to ensure that the university would be more equipped to handle any similar situation in the future.

The first major revision involved improving communication during a crisis. One of the primary lessons learned from the shooting was that real-time information was essential for the swift and effective response of both campus security and law enforcement. In the heat of the moment, the university's communication systems struggled to keep up with the rapidly unfolding situation. As a result, FSU implemented a more streamlined and efficient emergency notification system, ensuring that alerts could be sent out quickly to all students, faculty, and staff. The system was integrated with text messaging, email, and social media platforms, allowing the university to reach everyone on campus simultaneously. This improvement was crucial for evacuating students and providing instructions during an emergency.

FSU also focused on revising its active shooter response protocols. The university recognized the importance of not only having a response plan but also ensuring that it was regularly practiced and updated. In the past, active shooter drills had been conducted on campus, but the response to this particular incident revealed weaknesses in the execution of those drills. In response, FSU introduced more realistic and frequent active shooter simulations, involving both campus security and local law enforcement. These drills now focused on enhancing coordination between these groups, ensuring that they could work seamlessly together to neutralize the threat while minimizing harm to bystanders.

The university also took steps to strengthen its physical security infrastructure. While campus security had responded quickly, the ability to contain and control the situation was limited by the lack of certain security measures. As a result, FSU invested in the installation of more advanced security systems, such as real-time surveillance cameras, metal detectors at key campus entry points, and reinforced doors in high-traffic buildings. The university also increased the number of trained security personnel stationed across the campus, especially in areas considered to be high-risk during busy hours.

Another critical area of revision was the role of campus faculty and staff in the emergency response process. While many professors and staff acted heroically to protect students during the crisis, it became clear that more training was needed to ensure that all faculty members were prepared to act during a crisis. FSU implemented mandatory training programs for faculty and staff, focusing on how to handle emergency situations, communicate effectively during a crisis, and assist students in securing shelter or evacuating the area. This training aimed to provide faculty with the tools and knowledge to respond quickly and appropriately in future emergencies.

Finally, FSU's emergency response protocol revision included improving the mental health and trauma response post-crisis. While physical security was a priority, the emotional and psychological well-being of the campus community needed more attention. The university expanded its counseling services, ensuring that students, faculty, and staff had access to immediate mental health support following a crisis. Long-term mental health care and trauma recovery programs were also developed to support the ongoing needs of those affected by the shooting.

The FSU shooting prompted a thorough reevaluation and revision of the university's emergency response protocols. From improving communication systems to increasing the frequency of active shooter drills and investing in better physical security measures, FSU took comprehensive steps to ensure its readiness in the face of future crises. These changes were essential in rebuilding the trust of the campus community and providing students, faculty, and staff with the tools and resources needed to feel safe and supported in the aftermath of such a devastating event.

Chapter 14
Resilience in Red and Gold

In the aftermath of the devastating shooting at Florida State University (FSU) on April 17, 2025, the resilience of the university's students, faculty, and staff became a defining feature of the recovery process. While the tragedy left an indelible mark on the community, it also sparked a powerful wave of unity, activism, and determination to bring about meaningful change. This chapter explores the inspirational stories of FSU's student body and faculty, highlighting how they came together to support one another, honor the victims, and take action to ensure that such a tragedy would not be repeated.

FSU's strength in the face of adversity was visible in the way its students and faculty united in their grief, turning pain into a driving force for positive change. From organizing vigils and memorials to advocating for stronger campus safety measures, the FSU community demonstrated an unwavering commitment to healing together. Through collective action, students, faculty, and staff not only found a sense of solidarity but also became a voice for change in the broader conversation surrounding gun violence and campus safety.

The chapter also highlights how FSU's students, many of whom had been directly affected by the shooting, became leaders in the movement for change. Empowered by their own experiences, they worked tirelessly to raise awareness about mental health, advocate for gun control, and push for reforms that would protect future generations of students. Their activism inspired others on campus and across the nation, showing that even in the face of immense tragedy, the spirit of resilience and the desire to create a better future could prevail.

Through stories of unity, activism, and perseverance, this chapter reflects the incredible strength of FSU's community and the lasting impact their efforts for change will have on future generations.

Inspirational Stories of Unity and Activism

In the wake of the Florida State University (FSU) shooting on April 17, 2025, the response from the university's students, faculty, and staff was a powerful testament to the strength of unity and activism in the face of tragedy. While the event left the campus community devastated, it also sparked a profound collective resilience that manifested in a wave of inspirational stories, where pain was transformed into a driving force for positive change. Students, many of whom were directly affected by the shooting, took the lead in advocating for reforms, honoring the victims, and raising awareness about issues such as gun violence, mental health, and campus safety.

One of the first acts of unity came in the form of student-led memorial services. Within hours of the tragedy, students organized candlelight vigils, public gatherings, and memorial events to honor the victims. These gatherings were not only a way to mourn and reflect but also a powerful show of solidarity. Students stood together, supporting each other in a shared moment of grief. Their collective action provided a sense of healing for many who felt isolated in their sadness. Through these efforts, the students made it clear that while the shooting had fractured their sense of safety, it would not break their spirit or resolve to move forward as a united community.

Following the immediate aftermath of the shooting, FSU students didn't just stop at memorializing the victims—they also became leaders in the fight for systemic change. Many of them channeled their grief into activism, pushing for reforms in gun control laws, campus security policies, and mental health resources. One of the most powerful outcomes of their activism was the creation of student-led initiatives advocating for stricter gun laws and increased support for mental health services on campuses across the country. The FSU student body worked together to organize protests, speak at public forums, and lobby local and national lawmakers for legislative changes that would prioritize the safety and well-being of students.

These student-led movements gained national attention, as their voices resonated far beyond the FSU campus. Survivors of the shooting, as well as their peers, used social media and public platforms to amplify their message, showing the world that they were not just victims of violence but powerful agents of change. The #FSUstrong hashtag became a symbol of both remembrance and resilience, gaining traction across social media platforms and becoming a rallying cry for students and activists nationwide.

Faculty members also played a critical role in supporting student activism and fostering an environment of healing. Professors and university staff participated in memorials, encouraged students to take part in advocacy work, and helped to create a space for students to process their trauma. Many faculty members, already dedicated to the well-being of their students, stepped up to provide additional support, whether through counseling or offering academic accommodations for those who were struggling. The sense of unity between faculty and students was essential in maintaining the strength of the community during such a difficult period.

Ultimately, the stories of unity and activism that emerged in the wake of the FSU tragedy serve as a powerful reminder of the resilience of individuals in the face of overwhelming adversity. The campus community refused to let the shooting define them negatively. Instead, they chose to honor the victims' memories by advocating for positive change, creating an environment of collective healing, and ensuring that the voices of those directly affected by the tragedy would be heard. Through their activism, the students of FSU set a powerful example of how communities can unite to not only cope with tragedy but also take decisive action toward a safer, more compassionate future.

The Strength of FSU's Student Body and Faculty in Overcoming Tragedy

The strength of Florida State University's (FSU) student body and faculty in overcoming the tragic shooting on April 17, 2025, was truly remarkable. Despite the deep emotional trauma and sense of fear that permeated the campus, the collective resilience of both students and faculty became a cornerstone of the recovery process. Their ability to come together in solidarity, support one another, and transform their grief into a force for change highlighted the strength of the university community in the face of adversity.

In the days immediately following the shooting, the FSU student body demonstrated extraordinary unity. Students, many of whom were directly affected by the tragedy, rallied around each other, offering support and comfort during a time of immense pain. The campus, once a place of carefree academic and social life, became a space for collective grieving. Candlelight vigils, memorials, and gatherings were organized by students, not just to mourn the loss of their peers but also to reaffirm the strength of the community. These events allowed students to share their grief, express their solidarity, and honor the victims. Students leaned on one another, drawing strength from their shared experiences and finding a sense of collective healing in the midst of devastation.

Faculty members also played a pivotal role in the healing process. Professors and staff, who had witnessed the aftermath of the shooting and who were equally impacted by the violence, took on the responsibility of guiding their students through the emotional toll of the tragedy. Many professors offered emotional support and reassurance, providing safe spaces in classrooms for students to talk about their feelings. Some faculty members took it upon themselves to help students navigate the complex emotions of grief and fear, while others helped organize memorials and offered resources for counseling. This commitment to supporting students both academically and emotionally was a testament to the faculty's dedication to the well-being of their students, reinforcing the importance of community during difficult times.

The emotional strength demonstrated by both the student body and faculty in the aftermath of the tragedy was further demonstrated in their determination to advocate for change. Students, especially those who survived the shooting, became vocal advocates for improved campus safety, stronger mental health services, and reforms in gun control laws. Faculty members supported these efforts, encouraging students to use their voices to push for policy changes that would make campuses safer and prevent future tragedies. The partnership between students and faculty in these efforts was a powerful reflection of the shared sense of responsibility to ensure the safety and well-being of the entire campus community.

In addition to advocacy, the strength of the FSU community was evident in their commitment to rebuilding their sense of safety and normalcy. The university worked together to enhance campus security, improve mental health resources, and foster a supportive environment where students felt safe to express their emotions and seek help. The collective healing process was not just about recovering from the immediate trauma but also about ensuring that FSU would be a place where students could thrive despite the lingering effects of the tragedy.

The strength of FSU's student body and faculty in overcoming the shooting tragedy was a testament to their resilience, unity, and determination. Their ability to support one another, turn grief into action, and work together to rebuild the campus was a powerful example of the human spirit's capacity to heal and persevere in the face of overwhelming adversity. The tragedy at FSU was a moment of profound loss, but the response of the community showed that, even in the darkest times, there is hope and strength in coming together as one.

How FSU Students Are Leading Efforts for Change

In the wake of the Florida State University (FSU) shooting on April 17, 2025, the students of FSU emerged as the driving force behind efforts for meaningful change, channeling their grief and trauma into activism. Their response to the tragedy went beyond personal healing, as they took up the mantle to advocate for systemic reforms that would enhance campus safety, address gun violence, and promote mental health awareness. The students' leadership in the aftermath of the shooting not only exemplified their resilience but also demonstrated the powerful role that young people can play in shaping the future.

One of the most notable ways FSU students led efforts for change was through their advocacy for stronger gun laws. Many students, especially survivors of the shooting, became outspoken advocates for gun control, using their personal experiences to call for policy reforms that would prevent future tragedies. They joined national movements, partnered with organizations such as Everytown for Gun Safety, and organized rallies and protests on campus to push for stricter gun laws. Their efforts included lobbying lawmakers to implement more stringent background checks, restrict the sale of high-capacity magazines and assault weapons, and enhance gun control measures at the state and federal levels. The students made it clear that their personal loss would not be in vain, and they used their voices to demand that lawmakers prioritize the safety of students across the country.

In addition to advocating for gun control, FSU students were instrumental in pushing for improvements to campus safety protocols. They called for increased security measures, including better training for campus security officers and more comprehensive emergency preparedness drills. Students demanded a stronger collaboration between campus security and local law enforcement to ensure that in the event of a crisis, the response would be swift and coordinated. Through these efforts, students aimed to create a safer environment on campus, where students could focus on their academic pursuits without the constant fear of violence.

Equally important in the students' efforts for change was their push for enhanced mental health services on campus. Students recognized that the tragedy had highlighted the need for better mental health support for students, particularly for those struggling with emotional distress or trauma. Many students, particularly those who had experienced the psychological aftermath of the shooting, became vocal advocates for expanding counseling services and creating more accessible mental health resources. They campaigned for increased funding for campus mental health programs and worked to break down the stigma surrounding mental health care. The students emphasized that addressing mental health was not only a preventative measure for violent behavior but also a crucial component of fostering overall well-being on campus.

FSU students also took their advocacy efforts to social media, where they used platforms like Twitter, Instagram, and TikTok to raise awareness about the issues affecting them and their peers. The #FSUstrong hashtag became a symbol of solidarity, grief, and resilience. Through social media, students shared their stories, connected with national organizations, and rallied others to join their cause. The viral nature of their messages ensured that the conversation around campus safety, gun control, and mental health reached a wider audience, both within and beyond the university.

In addition to these efforts, FSU students organized fundraising campaigns, memorial events, and educational forums to keep the conversation alive and ensure that the victims' lives were not forgotten. They worked closely with survivors, families of victims, and faculty to create spaces for dialogue, healing, and advocacy.

FSU students became the leaders in the fight for change in the aftermath of the shooting. Their activism was driven by a deep sense of responsibility to honor the victims, prevent future violence, and create a safer, more supportive environment on campus. Through their efforts, they demonstrated not only their resilience but also their ability to bring about change on a national level. Their leadership continues to serve as an inspiration for other student bodies and activists, proving that even in the face of tragedy, young people have the power to lead and effect meaningful change.

Chapter 15
From Tragedy to Advocacy

In the aftermath of the Florida State University (FSU) shooting on April 17, 2025, the survivors and families of the victims emerged as powerful voices for change, using their personal experiences to fuel advocacy efforts aimed at preventing future tragedies. Their courage in sharing their stories and channeling their grief into action sparked a broader movement that not only demanded justice for the lives lost but also sought to address the systemic issues that contributed to the violence. This chapter explores how survivors and families of the victims have become key figures in the fight for legislative change, advocating for stronger gun control laws, improved campus safety, and better mental health resources.

The survivors, many of whom were directly impacted by the shooting, found purpose in turning their pain into advocacy. They worked tirelessly to push for reforms that would make campuses safer and ensure that no other families would have to experience the same tragedy. Their efforts were joined by the families of the victims, who, in their grief, found strength in their desire to make the world safer for others. Together, they have become influential voices in the ongoing conversation about gun violence and public safety.

In addition to personal advocacy, legislative efforts have been a significant focus. Survivors and families have worked alongside lawmakers, pushing for changes in gun laws and advocating for stricter policies to prevent future violence. Advocacy groups have also played a vital role in fostering public awareness, helping to mobilize communities and ensure that the issue of gun violence remains a top priority for policymakers.

This chapter examines the role these survivors, families, and advocacy groups have played in reshaping the national conversation on gun violence and campus safety, highlighting the intersection of personal loss, public action, and legislative change in the pursuit of a safer future.

How Survivors and Families Are Using Their Voices to Drive Change

In the wake of the Florida State University (FSU) shooting on April 17, 2025, survivors and families of the victims have become powerful advocates for change, using their personal experiences to highlight the need for reform in gun laws, campus safety, and mental health support. Their voices have played a crucial role in shifting the national conversation on gun violence, turning their pain into a catalyst for action.

Survivors, many of whom suffered physical injuries or witnessed the horrific events, have been vocal in sharing their stories and demanding stronger protections for students. They've used public platforms to call attention to the emotional and psychological toll of mass shootings, emphasizing the need for greater mental health resources and support for survivors in the aftermath of violence. Through interviews, social media posts, and public speaking engagements, survivors have humanized the statistics and statistics-driven debates about gun violence, making it clear that these issues are personal, deeply felt, and urgent. They have not only advocated for improved campus security but have also highlighted the critical importance of mental health services for students, pushing for changes in how universities address psychological well-being.

Families of the victims, while grieving, have also stepped forward to share their pain and demands for justice. By participating in rallies, writing op-eds, and meeting with lawmakers, they have become tireless advocates for stricter gun control laws, including background checks and regulations on assault weapons. They have worked with advocacy groups to ensure that their loved ones' deaths were not in vain and have pushed for legal reforms to protect future generations. Their efforts have added weight to the national debate on gun violence, as they have called for the creation of stronger legislation to prevent future shootings and hold those responsible for the proliferation of firearms accountable.

Together, survivors and families of the victims have used their voices to drive systemic change, ensuring that the tragedy at FSU continues to fuel efforts for safer campuses and stricter gun laws.

Legislative Efforts to Prevent Future Tragedies

In the aftermath of the Florida State University (FSU) shooting on April 17, 2025, legislative efforts to prevent future tragedies gained significant momentum, with survivors, families of victims, and advocacy groups leading the charge for change. The tragedy underscored the urgent need for comprehensive gun control reforms and improvements to campus safety, and these efforts rapidly gained support at both the state and national levels. The key focus of these legislative efforts was to close gaps in existing laws and create new policies that would prevent mass shootings and better protect individuals on college campuses.

One of the primary legislative efforts that emerged after the FSU shooting was the call for stronger gun control laws. Survivors and families of the victims, along with advocacy groups, lobbied for universal background checks, which would make it more difficult for individuals with mental health issues or a history of violence to legally acquire firearms. The shooting revealed that Phoenix Ikner, the perpetrator, was able to legally purchase a firearm despite his signs of emotional distress and troubling behavior. This raised questions about the sufficiency of existing background checks, particularly regarding mental health evaluations. Advocacy groups, such as Everytown for Gun Safety and the Brady Campaign, pushed for laws that would include more comprehensive mental health screenings and close the loopholes in the current background check system, such as the gun show loophole that allows private sales without a background check.

Additionally, survivors and victim families advocated for restrictions on assault weapons and high-capacity magazines, arguing that these types of firearms enable shooters to cause greater harm in a shorter period. Many proposed a return to the federal assault weapons ban, which was in place from 1994 to 2004. Such a ban would limit the availability of firearms with high firepower, making it more difficult for individuals to carry out mass shootings. Legislative efforts also included mandatory waiting periods for gun purchases, which would allow law enforcement to thoroughly assess potential buyers and provide a cooling-off period for individuals who may act impulsively.

Another critical aspect of the legislative response was focused on enhancing campus safety measures. Many proposed laws aimed to increase funding for security infrastructure on campuses, including surveillance systems, more visible security personnel, and more comprehensive training for campus security officers. These measures would ensure that universities are better equipped to handle emergency situations and respond more quickly in the event of a crisis. Furthermore, some student organizations pushed for laws that would regulate concealed carry on college campuses. They argued that allowing more weapons on campuses could increase the risks of accidental shootings or confusion during a live shooter situation. Campus safety reforms thus became a key area of focus for legislative action.

At the state level, lawmakers began introducing bills to address gun violence specifically in schools and on university campuses. Some states moved toward tightening restrictions on who could carry firearms in public spaces, particularly on educational property. Meanwhile, others proposed more resources for mental health programs on campuses, which would allow students to access counseling and support services before their mental health challenges escalated into crises.

Despite these efforts, passing comprehensive gun control laws at the federal level faced significant opposition, particularly from Second Amendment advocates and powerful lobbying groups like the National Rifle Association (NRA). These groups often argue that tighter regulations infringe on individual rights and that the focus should instead be on improving mental health care and ensuring that existing laws are properly enforced. However, the strength of the advocacy efforts following the FSU shooting, particularly from those who had directly experienced the trauma of gun violence, kept the issue in the public eye, leading to more conversations about reasonable reforms.

The legislative efforts to prevent future tragedies like the FSU shooting have been multifaceted, addressing everything from gun control reforms to campus safety and mental health services. While significant progress has been made in some areas, the struggle for comprehensive change remains ongoing. Survivors, victim families, and advocacy groups continue to push for laws that will make campuses safer and prevent further gun violence, ensuring that the tragedy at FSU serves as a turning point in the national conversation about gun control and public safety.

The Role of Advocacy Groups in Fostering Public Awareness

In the wake of the Florida State University (FSU) shooting on April 17, 2025, advocacy groups played an instrumental role in fostering public awareness about the issues surrounding gun violence, campus safety, and the need for legislative reform. These organizations became essential in amplifying the voices of survivors and victim families, ensuring that their calls for change were heard not only within the FSU community but also across the nation. By mobilizing public support and working closely with lawmakers, advocacy groups helped turn the grief from the tragedy into a powerful movement for meaningful change.

One of the primary roles of advocacy groups in the aftermath of the FSU shooting was to raise awareness about the relationship between gun violence and public safety. National organizations such as Everytown for Gun Safety, the Brady Campaign, and the Giffords Law Center to Prevent Gun Violence quickly aligned themselves with survivors and families of the victims, offering support and resources to help amplify their voices. These groups used their platforms to draw attention to the need for stricter gun laws, including universal background checks, assault weapon bans, and waiting periods for firearm purchases. They educated the public on the flaws in existing gun laws and the loopholes that allowed dangerous individuals to access firearms, thereby increasing the likelihood of tragedies like the one at FSU.

Advocacy groups also focused on the issue of campus safety, using the FSU shooting as an opportunity to push for better security protocols on university campuses. They highlighted the vulnerabilities of open college environments, where students are often unprotected and ill-prepared for an active shooter situation. Through public awareness campaigns, these organizations called for increased funding for campus security, better training for campus police, and more robust emergency response plans. They also worked to raise awareness about the importance of mental health services for students, advocating for better access to counseling and psychological support before individuals reach a crisis point.

Another critical area where advocacy groups made a difference was in challenging the stigma around mental health. In many cases, the shooters involved in mass shootings were individuals who exhibited signs of mental distress before resorting to violence. Advocacy groups pushed for public discussions about mental health, emphasizing that addressing psychological issues before they escalate into violent behavior could significantly reduce the likelihood of mass shootings. They advocated for greater funding for mental health programs on campuses and in communities, highlighting that access to mental health care was just as important as physical safety measures.

Social media was another tool that advocacy groups used effectively to raise awareness and mobilize support. Through platforms like Twitter, Instagram, and Facebook, these groups spread information, organized petitions, and called for national attention on the issue of gun violence and campus safety. The hashtag #FSUstrong quickly became a rallying cry for those advocating for change, spreading beyond FSU's campus and resonating with individuals nationwide. Social media also allowed survivors, families, and other affected individuals to share their stories, humanizing the statistics surrounding gun violence and making the issue more relatable to a broader audience.

Perhaps most importantly, advocacy groups acted as intermediaries between the public and lawmakers. They helped to ensure that the stories of survivors and victims' families reached policymakers, keeping the pressure on government officials to take action. Advocacy groups worked tirelessly to organize lobbying efforts, protests, and meetings with legislators to push for stronger gun control laws, improved campus safety regulations, and better mental health support systems. By providing survivors and families with the tools to navigate the political landscape, these groups empowered them to take their experiences and turn them into a force for legislative reform.

Advocacy groups played a crucial role in fostering public awareness and driving the national conversation about gun violence, campus safety, and mental health following the FSU shooting. Through their advocacy efforts, they helped transform the grief and trauma of the tragedy into a movement for change, pushing for reforms that would make campuses safer and protect future generations of students. Their efforts continue to be a vital force in the ongoing battle for stronger gun laws and improved campus security, ensuring that the voices of those affected by violence are heard and acted upon.

Part V

The National Impact

Chapter 16
Echoes Across America

The tragic shooting at Florida State University (FSU) on April 17, 2025, reverberated far beyond the FSU campus, sparking a national conversation about gun violence, campus safety, and the need for comprehensive reform. As the horror of this event unfolded, it became clear that the issues raised by the shooting were not unique to FSU but were part of a larger, troubling pattern of violence on college campuses across America. This chapter explores the national impact of the FSU shooting, drawing parallels to other school shootings and examining how this tragedy contributed to the growing movement for gun control and school safety reform.

The FSU shooting was a stark reminder of the vulnerability that students and faculty face on campuses nationwide. As communities around the country processed their grief and horror in the wake of the event, many saw the parallels with other recent tragedies. From Sandy Hook Elementary to Parkland, Florida, and beyond, the recurring nature of gun violence in schools highlighted the systemic issues that allowed such tragedies to continue. These parallels fueled a growing national movement advocating for change, with survivors, families, and activists calling for legislative reforms to address gun laws, mental health care, and campus security.

Moreover, this chapter examines how other universities responded to the FSU shooting and similar tragedies. Universities across the country began re-evaluating their own campus safety protocols, mental health services, and emergency response strategies. The lessons learned from the FSU shooting spurred widespread efforts to enhance security and ensure that students felt safe in their learning environments. As the movement for gun control and school safety reform gained momentum, the response to the FSU shooting became part of a larger, collective push for change, one that aimed to prevent future tragedies and create safer campuses nationwide.

The National Impact and Parallels with Other School Shootings

The tragic shooting at Florida State University (FSU) on April 17, 2025, resonated far beyond the campus, reverberating across the nation and drawing stark parallels with other school shootings that have tragically become part of the American landscape. The event not only shocked the FSU community but also reignited the conversation about the prevalence of gun violence in educational institutions and the systemic issues that continue to allow such tragedies to occur. It underscored the urgent need for reform in gun laws, campus security, and mental health support, reflecting a broader pattern of violence that has plagued schools in the U.S.

The parallels between the FSU shooting and other mass shootings at educational institutions are undeniable. Similar to the shooting at Parkland's Marjory Stoneman Douglas High School in 2018, where a shooter with a history of behavioral issues was able to gain access to firearms, the FSU shooting raised questions about how individuals with signs of mental distress or violent tendencies are able to legally obtain guns. The lack of adequate preventive measures and mental health support systems in place before the attack was echoed in previous tragedies, where warning signs were missed, and the potential for intervention was ignored or inadequately addressed.

The tragedy also mirrored the events at Sandy Hook Elementary in 2012, where young children were targeted, leaving the nation devastated and demanding action. Just as the shooting at Sandy Hook led to widespread calls for stricter gun control laws, the FSU incident contributed to the growing chorus of voices advocating for legislative change. Students, survivors, families, and advocacy groups across the country began to draw direct links between the lack of comprehensive gun regulation and the continued occurrence of school shootings, calling for universal background checks, assault weapons bans, and restrictions on high-capacity magazines.

In addition to gun control, the FSU shooting highlighted the broader issue of campus security. The lessons learned from the FSU incident paralleled the ongoing efforts to strengthen security at schools and universities nationwide. In the wake of the tragedy, universities began re-examining their emergency response plans, investing in improved surveillance systems, increasing campus security presence, and conducting regular active shooter drills. These reforms were modeled after the post-incident changes seen at other institutions that had been impacted by similar violence, such as Virginia Tech University after the 2007 shooting, where the response and security measures were extensively analyzed and improved.

The FSU shooting served as a stark reminder that these issues are not isolated but part of a much larger epidemic of gun violence affecting schools and universities across the United States. The emotional and psychological toll of these repeated tragedies has only fueled a growing national movement calling for change, not just in laws but in the culture surrounding gun violence and campus safety. As survivors and families of the victims of previous shootings joined forces with those affected by the FSU tragedy, their collective voices became a powerful force for reform.

The national impact of the FSU shooting highlighted the troubling parallels between this incident and other school shootings across the U.S. These repeated tragedies emphasized the urgent need for systemic change in gun laws, campus security measures, and mental health interventions. The growing movement for reform, spurred by the survivors and advocates of these events, seeks to break the cycle of violence that has become all too familiar in American schools and ensure that no more students, teachers, or families will have to face such unimaginable loss.

The Growing Movement for Gun Control and School Safety Reform

In the wake of the Florida State University (FSU) shooting on April 17, 2025, the growing movement for gun control and school safety reform gained significant momentum. The tragedy, like many mass shootings before it, reignited conversations about the intersection of gun violence, public safety, and the protection of students on campuses. While gun violence in schools and public spaces has become a disturbing pattern in the United States, events like the FSU shooting have sparked a stronger, unified response for reform across the nation, pushing for comprehensive changes that address both the accessibility of firearms and the preparedness of institutions to prevent such incidents.

One of the most significant aspects of the movement that emerged after the FSU shooting was the renewed call for stricter gun control laws. The tragedy once again highlighted the ease with which individuals, even those with troubling behavioral histories, can acquire firearms. Survivors, families of victims, and advocacy groups, including organizations like Everytown for Gun Safety, the Brady Campaign, and Moms Demand Action, immediately mobilized to demand legislative change. These groups pushed for stricter background checks, including more rigorous screening for mental health issues and behavioral red flags, as a way to prevent individuals at risk of violence from purchasing guns. The issue of assault weapons also resurfaced, with many advocating for a ban on high-powered firearms and high-capacity magazines, which have been a common tool used in mass shootings.

In addition to gun control, there was a strong push for reforming campus safety protocols. The FSU shooting, like many previous tragedies, highlighted the vulnerability of educational institutions to violent acts. Campus security measures and emergency response plans came under intense scrutiny, with many advocates calling for better-trained security personnel, increased visibility of campus police, and more effective emergency response systems. The tragic events at FSU reinforced the idea that universities need to be better prepared to handle active shooter situations, prompting discussions about how to improve coordination between campus security and local law enforcement.

Beyond physical security, the movement for school safety reform also emphasized the importance of mental health services and early intervention programs. Advocates argued that colleges and universities must prioritize mental health care, providing students with access to counseling and resources to address their emotional and psychological needs before crises escalate. The FSU tragedy, like previous school shootings, pointed to the critical role of mental health in preventing violence. Many argued that improving mental health screenings, particularly for those who may exhibit violent tendencies, could serve as a key preventive measure.

The growing movement for gun control and school safety reform also benefited from the increasing influence of student activists. In the aftermath of the FSU shooting, many students, particularly those who had survived the tragedy, became vocal advocates for change. They took to social media, participated in marches, and met with lawmakers, demanding stronger gun regulations and greater campus safety. The FSU shooting thus became part of a broader movement—one that had already gained traction following events like the Parkland shooting in 2018. Young people, many of whom are directly impacted by the violence, have become some of the most passionate voices in pushing for legislative change, showing that activism can create lasting impact.

The FSU shooting played a pivotal role in driving the growing movement for gun control and school safety reform. It underscored the need for comprehensive changes, including stricter gun laws, improved campus security measures, and better mental health resources. As survivors, students, faculty, and advocacy groups continue to push for legislative reforms, their efforts highlight a critical turning point in the national conversation about how to protect students and prevent future tragedies. With increasing public support and activism, this movement aims to create a safer environment for future generations, ensuring that the voices of those affected by gun violence are heard and acted upon.

How Other Universities Are Responding to Similar Tragedies

In the wake of the Florida State University (FSU) shooting, many other universities across the country began to reevaluate and revise their safety protocols, mental health support services, and overall emergency preparedness plans. The tragedy underscored the need for comprehensive campus safety measures and comprehensive mental health programs that could prevent similar events from occurring. FSU's experience, along with previous campus shootings, has prompted a nationwide shift in how universities approach campus security, student well-being, and emergency response procedures.

Universities around the United States are revisiting their campus security policies to address the increasing threat of violence. Many institutions have adopted more stringent security measures, including increased surveillance, enhanced access control systems, and the presence of more security personnel in high-traffic areas. At some schools, this has involved adding metal detectors, security checkpoints, or even campus-wide bag checks to prevent the entry of weapons. In addition to these measures, universities have been investing in more sophisticated communication systems that allow for instant mass notifications in case of an emergency. These systems are critical for informing students and faculty about an active shooter situation, providing real-time updates, and helping individuals make informed decisions about their safety.

Moreover, the tragedy at FSU and similar events have highlighted the urgent need for universities to bolster their mental health services. Institutions are increasingly focused on providing accessible counseling and support programs for students, staff, and faculty who may be affected by trauma, anxiety, or grief. Many schools have expanded their counseling departments, hired additional mental health professionals, and made it easier for students to access therapy sessions without lengthy waiting periods. Additionally, some universities are implementing programs aimed at early intervention, where students can seek help for mental health concerns before they escalate into crises.

To further prevent violence, many universities are revising their training programs for both faculty and students. Training for faculty now often includes recognizing signs of mental distress in students, how to intervene, and where to direct students for support. Some universities are offering workshops or seminars for students to help them understand how to report suspicious behavior or threats and how to be proactive in protecting their community. Campus-wide drills and simulations are becoming more common, ensuring that students and staff are prepared for potential crises and understand how to respond effectively during emergencies.

In the aftermath of tragic shootings, many universities have also established memorials, held vigils, and provided support for victims' families, reflecting the importance of community healing. Campuses have come together, not only to honor those who have lost their lives but also to support one another through shared grief. This communal response to tragedy often fosters solidarity and creates an environment where healing can begin.

On the legislative front, some universities have become more involved in advocating for national and local gun safety laws and campus safety reforms. Recognizing that the conversation around campus shootings extends beyond their own campuses, universities have joined forces with advocacy groups to push for stricter gun control measures, including universal background checks, assault weapon bans, and regulations to limit the accessibility of firearms to individuals with histories of violence or mental health issues.

Universities across the country have responded to campus tragedies by reevaluating their safety protocols, investing in mental health services, improving emergency preparedness, and fostering a culture of activism and prevention. The lessons learned from the tragedies at FSU, Virginia Tech, and other schools have driven campuses to implement tangible changes that prioritize student safety, well-being, and community healing. These changes reflect the broader societal shift towards preventing violence in schools and ensuring that students can learn and thrive in safe, supportive environments. As these efforts continue, they underscore the commitment of educational institutions to not only protect students but to create environments where individuals feel supported and empowered to reach out for help before tragedy strikes.

Epilogue
The Union Remains

In the aftermath of the devastating shooting at Florida State University (FSU) on April 17, 2025, the road to healing has been long, but the resilience displayed by the campus community has been unwavering. The tragedy, while leaving an indelible mark on those directly affected, also ignited a collective drive for change. This chapter, "The Union Remains," reflects on the journey of grief, recovery, and advocacy that has unfolded in the wake of the shooting, highlighting the resilience of the FSU community and the efforts to create a safer environment for future generations of students.

The FSU shooting exposed deep flaws in campus security, gun control, and mental health services, but it also catalyzed profound reforms and an outpouring of activism. Survivors, families, faculty, and students rallied together to ensure that the legacy of those lost would not be defined by violence, but by the strength and determination of the community to prevent future tragedies. Their efforts, driven by grief but fueled by a desire to protect others, have led to significant changes in policies, laws, and attitudes toward gun violence and campus safety.

As the university continues to recover, this chapter reflects on the ongoing work to build a safer, more supportive campus environment. It examines how FSU's resilience has set an example for other institutions, showing that, while healing from such a tragedy is a slow process, it is possible to turn grief into lasting change. Looking toward the future, FSU's commitment to preventing further violence and fostering a culture of safety and support remains strong, ensuring that the memory of the victims will continue to inspire a safer and more compassionate educational experience for all. The union of FSU's community stands as a testament to the power of unity, resilience, and the unyielding pursuit of change.

Final Reflections on Grief, Resilience, and Creating Safer Campuses

The tragic shooting at Florida State University (FSU) left an indelible mark on the campus community. In the wake of this devastating event, the process of grieving was painful, but it was also accompanied by remarkable acts of resilience. The tragedy forced students, faculty, and staff to confront the brutal reality of campus violence, but it also ignited a collective determination to rebuild and ensure that no future student would have to endure the same pain. The grief was profound and deeply personal for many, yet it transformed into a driving force for change. The FSU community, though shaken to its core, emerged stronger, united in their resolve to prevent such violence from occurring again.

Grief, as experienced by survivors and the families of victims, was not simply about the loss of life but also the loss of innocence and a sense of safety that is supposed to be inherent in an academic environment. Students who once walked the FSU campus without fear now found themselves grappling with anxiety, loss of trust, and an overwhelming sense of vulnerability. However, through shared mourning, collective action, and a determination to honor the victims' memories, the campus slowly began to heal. Survivors became vocal advocates for change, channeling their pain into activism that called for stronger gun control, better campus security, and more mental health resources for students.

The resilience displayed by the FSU community—students, faculty, and staff alike—became the foundation for meaningful reform. In the aftermath, there was an outpouring of solidarity and support, not only within the FSU community but also from across the country. Students took leadership roles, advocating for safer campuses, gun control laws, and improved mental health care. Their voices, amplified by their personal experiences, became a powerful force for legislative change. This activism provided a sense of purpose and healing, turning grief into tangible efforts aimed at preventing future violence.

In the context of creating safer campuses, the FSU shooting underscored the need for institutions of higher learning to reassess their security protocols, mental health support systems, and emergency preparedness plans. The lessons learned from the tragedy became a catalyst for widespread change. Universities across the country began to adopt more comprehensive safety measures, including better surveillance, more visible security, and improved coordination with local law enforcement. More attention was given to mental health services, with universities striving to ensure that students had access to the counseling and care they needed before reaching a crisis point.

Looking ahead, FSU's journey toward healing and reform is far from over. The legacy of the victims lives on, not just in the memories of those who knew them, but in the continued efforts for campus safety and violence prevention. The work of survivors, families, students, and faculty has already led to concrete changes, but the fight for safer campuses continues. By sharing their stories and advocating for policy change, the FSU community has transformed grief into a powerful call for a future where students can learn and grow without fear of violence. The resilience and activism sparked by this tragedy will continue to shape the university's commitment to ensuring the safety and well-being of all students for generations to come.

The Legacy of FSU's Resilience and the Continuing Efforts for Change

The legacy of Florida State University's (FSU) resilience is defined not only by the strength of its response to tragedy but also by the ongoing efforts for meaningful change that have emerged from it. In the wake of the devastating shooting, the campus community—comprising students, faculty, staff, and families—united in grief and solidarity, transforming their collective pain into advocacy for change. The memory of those lost and the experiences of those directly affected became the driving force behind a national movement for gun control, campus safety reform, and better mental health support systems.

FSU's resilience was evident in how the university rebuilt trust among its students, faculty, and staff. Survivor-led movements called for stricter gun laws, better campus security measures, and improved mental health services, all of which became central to the university's recovery efforts. This movement quickly gained national traction, and survivors of the tragedy worked alongside advocacy groups to raise awareness and push for legislative reforms at both the state and national levels. Their voices became part of a larger conversation on gun violence and its devastating impact on communities, including schools and universities.

The university's commitment to safety and prevention became evident in the structural changes made to enhance campus security. These reforms included improving emergency response protocols, expanding mental health services, and fostering a more supportive environment for students. FSU's approach became a model for other institutions, showing that healing is not just about recovering from the trauma of a single event but about transforming that pain into a long-term commitment to safety and reform.

The continuing efforts for change represent a lasting legacy of resilience. While the scars of the tragedy remain, the determination to ensure a safer and more supportive environment for future students reflects the unbreakable spirit of the FSU community. Through collective action and a shared commitment to change, FSU's resilience serves as an example for other campuses and communities seeking to prevent further violence and ensure that such tragedies never happen again.

Looking Toward a Future of Healing and Protection

Looking toward a future of healing and protection, Florida State University (FSU) has committed itself to creating an environment where students can thrive academically, emotionally, and physically without the threat of violence. The tragedy that shook the FSU community prompted a series of changes aimed at ensuring that future generations of students will be better protected, supported, and cared for. As the healing process continues, the university is focused not only on improving physical security but also on fostering a culture of empathy, mental well-being, and shared responsibility.

One of the most crucial aspects of this vision is the strengthening of campus security. FSU has implemented measures to enhance surveillance, increase the presence of trained security officers, and ensure better communication between campus security and law enforcement. These measures are designed to create a safer campus environment, where students and faculty can go about their daily lives without the constant fear of violence. Additionally, improved emergency protocols, including more frequent and realistic active shooter drills, ensure that everyone on campus is better prepared for any crisis.

Equally important is the university's focus on mental health and emotional well-being. The FSU community has recognized that healing is not just about physical safety; it is about supporting the mental and emotional health of students, faculty, and staff. The expansion of counseling services, peer support programs, and mental health awareness campaigns demonstrates the university's commitment to ensuring that students have the resources they need to thrive. Mental health is now seen as integral to overall student success, and FSU has worked hard to remove the stigma surrounding it.

www.ingramcontent.com/pod-product-compliance
Lightning Source LLC
LaVergne TN
LVHW061528070526
838199LV00009B/417